When I Do Changes
Living in a changing world
Volume 1

J. W. Christian

COPYRIGHT © 2024 BY J.W. Christian.

All right reserved.

Acknowledgment:

As I press upon you my heartfelt thoughts, I am encouraged and overwhelmed with joy that I can take this moment to congratulate you on a job well done. With your help, I am prepared to do magnificent work in the Lord. You helped change my mind and lifestyle through the presence of the Lord through your living for Christ.

All saints are shining examples of who the Lord can take from nothing and make into something that others will enjoy and appreciate. Your knowledge and strength have helped open doors that were closed; therefore, I take this time to say thanks with all my heart, soul, and mind. I am thankful for you.

To the family that stood by me through my thirty plus years in the military, I say thank you from my heart. The journey was long but worth it. You are the beneficiary of a great deed, and I applaud you from the depth of my heart.

To my daughters, Heather and Demetrius, and sons, Jermeitrick and Theron: I applaud each of you for your dedication. I thank you for your unconditional love that supported me through the years—through those school days I missed and through those days you prayed for me, I felt the presence of the Lord upon me, and I thank you for the family love that you showed and helped me to understand. You have provided me with boundless joy and memories I can revisit forever.

To the entire church body of Christ: this is a glorious day that I can stand and shout out to you, "The Lord has given me great measure pressed down and runneth over." I give Him high praise for allowing us to meet and blend as a family, to be there for each other, and to grow together in Christ, who strengthens us.

It is nice to know that love was there for me, and through love and prayers, I stood firm; I walked closer to the Lord. My daily walk with Him has brought me boundless joy through healing that I cherish each day. Through your prayers and fasting, I have overcome. I take this time to say thanks to everyone for your support and for helping me to live the fullness of Christ.

To the Lord my God who opened my eyes to see, feels, and loves again: I know the deed that Lord have afforded me. I know the sacrifice the Lord made for me and the mountains He turned into hills. The dry bones in the valley of my life that the Lord lifted me from and allowed me to rise again, I give thanks. I love the Lord from the depth of my heart with all my soul and mind. I thank Him for seeing something in me that I did not see in myself and allowing that vision to come forth. Lord my God, I thank Thee for bringing out the best of me from the darkness that was obsessed with my soul. I thank Thee for being patient with me and, walking me into the marvelous light and showing me there are better days ahead for me in my changes, men.

TABLE OF CONTENTS

Introduction _____ 1

    Divorce _____ 19

Chapter 1 God compassion and our Fears _____ 21

    The Lord is a Keeper _____ 29

    Forever Loving the Lord _____ 32

    Commitment of love _____ 36

    Footsteps of Love _____ 37

    A love that is real. _____ 40

    An oil painting of Love _____ 44

Chapter 2 Loving and Sharing _____ 49

    Active relationships come with devotion and with a purpose. ___ 54

    Christ's C/G=Center of Gravity _____ 55

    Love abides with you. _____ 63

    Breaking through _____ 70

Chapter 3 Damaged Goods _____ 78

Stop lying to yourself. 83

False liars 86

Reaching out and finding out 100

Why broken hearts bleed 103

Going to bed mad 110

A couple of pitfalls 117

My Prayer: 132

In the palm of darkness 133

Conscience Faults 144

Chapter 4 Not Putting the God First 150

Blind spots in a marriage 183

Emotional Baggage 188

Costly Sins 192

Scripture References: 198

Other studies: 198

INTRODUCTION

Roman 12: 21 Be not overcome of evil but overcome evil with good.

There is some good in everyone you just must know where to look.

Divorce can bring out the ugly in a person.

"If you never correct what is wrong before you say I-Do, things will continue to go wrong after you say I-Do."

This book is not about sorting out who is at fault in their divorce or marriage that caused the separation that led to divorce. But, it is designed to determine errors and mistakes surrounding each marriage that kick off separate procedures. There is a breaking point in every marriage that causes them to max out and cross blurred lines. These pushes, crossfire, and limitation cause the edge to go beyond its breaking point.

Sometimes, we do not understand what our own fears are doing or can do to us, so we take off running with yesterday's problems in tow. Because we take our act on the road or involve other people in our decision-making process we end up with other people in our business. We uproot our common sense and walk around feeling used and abused by wearing our hurt on our shoulder barking at the world.

Each person is responsible for their own actions, thoughts, and beliefs. Sometimes, we live by what we learn from others and that becomes our example for living the way we do and justify our actions. We should look for ways to redeem our marriage or our marriage by working hard to make it work, but that is not always possible to do. When a spouse does not want you, they just do not want you, no matter what you do, to encourage the marriage to continue in a positive direction.

When the love of your life is in and out of your heart, it is hard to comprehend what the heart is saying, you will find yourself chasing time. We must realize that marriage is a solemn, lifetime commitment. We can live more successfully if we enter marriage carefully, firmly making up our mind that this marriage is for keeps. I am here to let you know that you are no different from any other person that is going through or has been through a divorce or in the final stages of their divorce or a crushing marriage. The Lord sees your pain and hurt, for he is not blind. He sees the tears in your eyes, spots, and places where you are struggling to hold on.

One night of crying, two days of thinking about all the things that occurred between your lacks understanding had fail to make sense why your spouse's attitude about leaving had left you in an uproar. Yet, by the end of the day, you still have no clue because your marriage is over. He sees and feels the shadows of your mind rushing back through time only to end up fighting the pain of yesterday, now that you see the handwriting on the wall, read it and obey.

If you are afraid to look back, you will never see your future. You got to know where you been, to see where you are going to know where you need to be. You never thought divorce would be a day that would be so sad. You closed off your mind and all the things that you ever thought hurt now.

You thought you would walk around and have things your way. He sees the isolation that forced you to separate your love that created your suffering that you are going through. Though you may not have a shoulder to lean on and no arms to hold you or simply understand that you can still stand strong. No one can tell you any different when you are giving an account of your own actions and crises.

Couple's must be willing to share and be willing to share their innermost feels and, at the same time, face the fact that love, love them no more through the eyes that once love them. A broken heart forced you to face the fact that you are living with a broken heart that is difficult to heal but can be healed. You are an open wound with all the healing power in the world in your hand to see through the rainbow to view the end of the storm.

Knowing love is better than having gold or silver because your love is not less than precious rubies. The heartbeat of the heart chambers is full of love that is unique to the heart itself. In-love or being in-love with someone other than yourself will bring out new moment in your life that will magnify happiness in your life that will pour out from the soul to press upon your body to bring out the best in you. Love expresses new ways and tilts the justice of the heart.

Love brings out the best in you because love can be express in countless ways because you have someone to share your life with that will open a floodgate of opportunity for love. Love is someone that can see you for who you are and hold a valve that praiseworthy of your love to give it back in returned. And all that is good in you that equal happiness is giving to an individual heart without looking for something in return.

For what you have in love is more than joy for our soul. Love is willing to go the extra mile to exist in your life. Love believes and lives on the notion that the heart will always be there for you every step of the way. I see a future that is so precious that trying to live it without you would be impossible to do. I cannot see myself with anyone else but you. A blind man can see my heart, and I confessing my love to you, and you are my only desire. When I need someone to lift my spirits you are there for me when the chips are down, and I am feeling at my lowest.

You gave me that feeling that I belonged to someone that is special. I found that special someone to be you. I love you for who you are and for what you stand. I love you because you believed in your dreams and using all your resources to complete them to the best of your ability. I see what you see because I believe in you and the dreams that you are seeking. I see gifts and talents the Lord has blessed you with to help you to grow and overcome your troubles.

Heaven has made a great investment in your soul that the Lord has let you enjoy. I thank the Lord for understanding my desire to be happy. Lord thank you for giving me the knowledge I was in a dark place, and you became my light that I can walk by, that I can see by, light by which I can live. The smile that you brought to my face is there forever because I see the glorious of your blessing shining upon me.

What a joy it is to be loved by you and to know that you saw sometime inside my heart and gave it true valve that money cannot buy or put a price on. The Lord knew you would be in situations that your heart and eyes would see no way out of. That he would need to be there for you through your heartaches and troublesome times.

The Lord gave us never ending love around-and-about-over, and under the cross, he gave up his life for you and me. Through his undying love, he experienced and released unconditional love to shower us. He opened his heart, reached into our heart, and brought out the best in us, and from the best in him, we can live and show the world how love work and how love through him to us we can share it with someone else that we love the same way. Love should be a shining example what love is and for others to see and experience.

The Lord creates love in us from his likeliness. The heart cannot overrule love because love is innate to be loved, and it must show and act in harmony. Couples choose not to love because they believed they will have to give too much of themselves back. When objects in our marriage surround us, we should see them for what they are. Couples should associate and show feels of emotion toward each other in a way that spells Christ love in them.

I believe in show and tell, there is no reason to stop loving someone because you or they are experiencing difficulties and facing hardship. I look at love with an open eye through the heart, soul, and mind. If I die and come back, I will ask the Lord for love to accompany me because I want to keep experience all that the Lord had for me to love. This is my lifetime wish, and I know the Lord will not fail me. The Lord's love is my world, my beginning and ending and without ever experiencing your love. I would never know how it feels to be absolutely loved and appreciated. My world would be empty like a bird without a nest; I would just fly aimless without purpose.

If I could put one word in a sentence and erases all the hurt and pain that I felt, I would use it to take away yesterday. Since I am not able to undo or turned back the hands of time. I must go through each day praying that things change. Receiving insight is one step in understanding God's plan for my life, but living within that vision is another? But at first, I did not see it that way, and I walked on my own accord. The Lord plans for marriage, and the family was in my hand pass down through his word. I need you to understand there is one ultimate answer to every question and all problems that you might encounter that may have escaped your mind.

In the inspiration word of the Lord, we are to seek the Lord way, and without him, we could be on a dead-end road or simple perished behind our own foolishness. It is up to us what choices we make through commitment in our marriage with each other. By begin an example, we can stand before the Lord with grace and mercy to claim our journey.

This applies to all who were created in such a way that they lone for a marriage with the creator. I know for sure when we are disconnected from the Lord's Grace and Mercy, we find ourselves behind the wheel of destruction. When we make a personal decided to go our own way and create our own Garden of Eden, we break the intimate marriage with the Lord.

Hard times come into marriage in one form or another, but it we can pray our way through our turmoil and hold on to God unchanging hand. By doing this, we are allowed to stand the test of time and grow stronger through the atoning of God blessings. When we stand and weather the storm, and when everything seems wrong, we can still stand and fight off the evildoers of your life.

We do not have to live or give in to pressure we can stop and be blessed on the ground that we do not have to run and hide from our faults. It your life, so take the time to step up to the plate, and everything will be all right if you put the Lord first in your marriage.

Couples need to stick together and be as one where their testimony will speak highly of them. While others are playing hiding-go seek, your action will speak of your commitment to the Lord, and other's will see the work the Lord is doing in you. As they shout their trouble over others will see and believe the witness report.

The most fruitful and healthy way to manage any situation is to stay and be opened mind that the Lord is working thing out in your favor. This way, you will have a backbone and a foundation to stand on. Having someone you can talk to and produce a solution that will lead to a promising marriage in Christ who will understand your crisis and who can help you overcome your calamities.

When love is alive and well, others can see it clear as the morning dew flashing as the morning sun rise. Looking at your problems and trying to eliminate any irritating behavior that might be misaligning you with the Lord is a plus in your favor. Keeping the Lord's plan in heart and your eyes on the sparrow can lead you through impossible and strengthen you on your daily journey. A marriage will work out if both parties are working with the same goals in mind and be willing to go the extra mile to walk in harmony with each other.

Developing a relationship before you say I-Do

Love represents who you are.

One of the fundamentals of any marriage and relationship is seeking to understand your counterpart before you say I-do. It is important to understand the measure of a relationship to develop a marriage that is fully functionally that will represent the presence of the Lord. By seeking the Lord first in a relationship, the measure of the marriage will be an endless supply of love and affection. Marriage will always come out on top, for the Lord sees marriage as a constitution of heaven (make in heaven, written by the laws of heaven, therefore governor by heaven).

A husband said: After the honeymoon night was over during the wee hours of the morning, his newlywed woke up and asked him a question. Are you going to love me forever? He lay there silently as possible, as if he did not hear her. A moment later, he closed his eyes and rolled over, his wife nudged him in the side. He sits up on the side of the bed and walked over to the window and opened it. He starts counting stars. His wife jumped out of bed and ran over to him and put her arms around him, and said Baby, baby, it will take you forever to count all those stars. He slowly turned to her and said that how long I will love you, forever.

At some point, before you say I-D, a question needs to be asked is this really what I want and need in my life to make my life and what I dream complete. There is one question that needs to be asked up front, not after the fact. I know forever is a long time, but can you ask your spouse too much if they would love you forever. Will you watch our love hurt struggle, will you pay attention or abuse our love and causes us to suffer? Will our love overlook our mistakes or take advantage of every opportunity to shine amid darkness that we both can see our way back to each other? It your choices, your life to live, your decision, you decide, what our love should look like and be.

Few words will be expressed between couples after a misunderstanding has taken place. Sometimes, the bridge gap can be more than just a walk in the park. Most misunderstanding occurs under the nature of sin and in the presence of closed-minded person and the bad attitudes of the person. After the doors to the marriage slapped closed, lies and abuse work together to turn minor problems into major problems in the marriage. While sin lays and waits for each moment to take place, the chaos sits patiently, waiting to seize it moment in that waits. The recovery stages for most couples are long and, in some cases, very painful.

As both couples start to withdraw from the presence of each other, turmoil between the two begin to focus on what causes the incident to occur, not how to overcome or keep it from occurring again. As life forces you to deal with situation and circumstance in your life circle, we become uncomfortable with our environment by seeking small and familiar outlets. Non-outlets will cause us to respond to negative inputs as well as causes us to walk blindfolded through our daily journey.

At some point, you will need to sit down with the Lord and talk with him about your situation. He has a soft voice that understands your heart, and his whispers will sit down with you and map out a plan that your heart understands. He had plans for us, but we do not listen with purpose. As the Lord speak to us in forms of paradigms, his action and daily bread, He freed us to strength us in a way that we become one in marriage and with him.

He used our journey as a stepping stone in our life that we might learn to share our thoughts and feelings to see the fullness of God's heart as he guides us through and out of our turmoil. As the Lord teaches us to sit down and talk thing out to follow his instructions and plans for our life, he opens our heart to feel for each other in ways that we never thought was possible. His goal for our life and living is simple and is placed up front for us to follow. The road is set and paved with the scale of life difficulties to lighten the load of injustice that we might face in our marriage.

Setting goals before you say I-Do be upfront and open about your goals:

Identify what direction you are going in and explain why they are important to you.

Identify and show why you think a relationship is important before marriage and why it is important for it to stand on solid ground.

Make sure your spouse is on the same page with you before turning it. In this step understanding is important to and in the marriage. (Never leave your spouse mindless, catching up is hard to do and giving up makes it easier to walk away.).

Set goals and plans that you both can achieve and live with and follow up on.

Seek positive outcome through understanding each other before you say-I-do.

Reward the relationship before marriage and continue after marriage by seeing the overall picture of the marriage and visit the vision (picture) often to stay focused.

Work with people who have similar goals (church, community) etc.

Deciding your goals:

Be honest with each other and make decisions together.

Do away with dangerous friendships by cutting them off.

Think of consequences as an alternative (be objective)

Avoid unhealthy and dangerous risks in the marriage (like negative friends who are always giving bad advice)

Work on strategies that best promote the marriage (like positive friends with clever ideas)

Keep goals in front of you by helping your spouse see the big picture.

Decide which goals work best for the marriage and work on them together.

Managing emotions is marriage:

Recognizing and seeing valve in your spouse can help you manage your emotions, and be open with yourself will help your spouse understand who you are and what they mean to you.

Combine and express your feelings with words through action use a show and tell method.

See mistakes as a learning experience, not an opportunity to hammer your spouse.

Sit down with your spouse and go over trouble spots that are causing you to hurdle over and out of your marriage.

Find common ground within the marriage to grow and neutralize outside forces that is causing doubt.

Seek to understand the triggers that create difference between what you say and how you express them (word phrases)

Determine what stresses you in the marriage and discuss ways to eliminate or a way to manage them.

Umbrella Love:

Stop trying to be someone you are not, just changed to what you should be.

Be there for each other and be each other's best friend/sounding board (if not, someone else will do your job for you)

Recognize and praise qualities you see in each other.

Work together on projects/one mind-one goal.

Practice learning how to socialize with each other (talk about anything and be open minded about it)

Help others by showing love toward one another and express love from the heart.

Celebrate each other differences/stop complaining about each other indifferences.

Be a reliable source for each other and be resourceful (study how to be pleasant/pleasure to each other.

Closing the communication gap:

Say what you need and what you want from the marriage/spouse/say it by making it clear.

Speak honestly openly but not hurtfully, remove any doubt of misunderstanding.

Ask questions that are open-ended that match open-mindedness.

Learn the language of your spouse, their body expression, and the tone of their voice.

Pay attention to your spouse's difficulties (especially that time of the month) learn them in a way that they become you and you them.

You can say no with understanding and be willing to disagree/agree to disagree.

Be open for suggestions and, be willing to reach inside your heart for understanding, and be not afraid to express your thoughts in a helpful way that promotes the relationship/marriage.

Conflict resolution:

Stop calling each other names, your spouse is what you called them.

Do not be competitive with your spouse there are things they can do better than you.

Demonstrate what you want and be willing to give suggestions as a solution.

Brainstorm with each other to unlock hidden treasures in the marriage.

Work on things in the marriage that your spouse is struggling with.

Talk about how to better understand each other openly/unchain your mind/think freely, and tear down any walls of confusion.

Describe what upsets you/your weaknesses/your strengths/use personal commitments as a method of understanding (I will do this) to understand and do better to complete the marriage.

Let the Lord stay in control of your marriage.

Do not take matters into your own hands.

Let the Lord order your steps.

"Praying together mean staying together, is seeing eye to eye, feeling and knowing each other where they are."

Worshiping together, attend church together, create a new and great relationship with each other, most important, loyalty, honesty, integrity. I trust that you are doing what you said you are doing; I believed you are where you say you are, having faith that you are what you say you are and nothing different about whom you are will come about that I can doubt your love for this marriage and commitment to it.

Another day without hearing from you

I see you every morning before my eyes open.

Dancing around in my head; pulling at my heart.

Like a flash of hope dangling from a smile.

I am starting my day off without hearing from you.

From thousands of miles of leftover pain

The trail is clear it is because of you that I hurt.

All the missed moments we shared together.

Most of all what we used to do.

Missing all the seconds under the moon light

You left me in this dark place in my life.

I been trying to get out, but I am trapped.

Talking about a touch,

How we learned so much about each other

Your love for me kept me from losing my mind.

Now, I cannot even touch, I am close to that again.

Back then, I saw our future, I must have to admit.

I did not see this coming at all.

I never knew love could hurt so badly.

Until that moment, I woke up without you

It has been another day without hearing from you.

I know how a crying heart feel.

Why a struggling heart have trouble healing.

If you know what I know

Then we are on the same page

We talked about each other's through our love

We showed each other a reflection of love

From that show case, we felt each other touch

All that is gone now,

Now we are at each other throat.

I speak about another; you talk about someone else

Our dreams of for others,

Neither one of us want each other

Like a bad headache, we struggle like that

My life is worthless without you.

Down on our knees, behind closed door

We are different people what the public see

We cannot stop touching each other.

It has been another day,

Another moment, another second

Without hearing from you

I am doing my best to keep hope alive.

Nothing about my heart

Being in love is fading away.

What are you doing to me?

My heart cannot take it.

I can hold on to another day,

Another day without hearing from you

O how I wish you were here with me

Waiting for my heart to beat

I am about to pass out.

From holding my breath

Please come through that door

Like broken glass and thousands of pieces

My dreams are slipping and falling away from me.

It has been an uphill struggle.

Without your love, I would simply float away

It has been another day without hearing from you.

I keep getting more.

And more confused should I go or stay.

My number address, you know by heart.

Nothing will change the love I feel for you.

I carry it with me each day.

I am learning to live.

Another day without hearing from you

Each marriage stands on its own merit. Individuals in a relationship make the marriage a workable relationship. It is not how big errors are in a relationship that causes it to crumble but the small pieces that make up the whole that never connect. Inside the heart of each couple, there is a tendency to cry independence, never finding the comfort to cry on each other shoulder. When the heart feel used and abused, it usually show up as floodgate of tears in the middle of a sunny day.

Every now and then, couples feel the pressure of missing something they never had in the relationship but never adjust to the need of the relationship. Some solutions in marriages are just thoughts that never get played out in the relationship because couples never seek opportunity to enhance their marriage. Eyes are doorways to the heart, which can be closed-off and filled with empty emotions that flow with negative thoughts that feed the flesh. In most cases, your heart is trying to love, but love is never given in return, so the heart gives what it had never received. Otherwise, the heart is not feeling what your eyes are seeing.

A heart can be disengaged in a marriage and cause great suffering because of its non-commitment to the marriage or their spouse. When you do not see or feel your heart will start to detach and cleave to unhealthy thoughts. When the mind fails to comprehend and stay in contact with itself, it loses the importance of touch and feeling. It is necessary to let the Lord wiped your weeping eyes and strengthen you through your weakness. The Lord will take away your pain and hurt where you can feel again. Because there will be days like this that the heart cannot stand being disconnected. I see no need for you to cry anymore when you can let go and let it be over with.

You cannot turn back the hands of time or undo yesterday. So why would you put yourself through difficulties when you have a source you can depend on that will understand and supply you with a better future. So, my child, cry no more, for I am here for you and with you, like always and forever. In your divorce, through your divorce, for your divorce, I am the one who will strengthen you. My words are simple and true I will never forsake you, nor would I leave you. I will be your spouse. Divorce is never an option I will consider.

"Divorce is like snowflakes there is never any two the same."

I never thought it would come to this.

What kind of friend would I be?

If I let you fall and stand there

And not reach down to help you.

We can chase our dreams together.

Win or lose, I will never let you down.

If you lean, I will lean against you.

Until you can stand again

There is so much love between us.

That our love creates palms, creeks, and trees.

Like melted ice and running water

The Lord would be proud of us.

For we tried so hard

To mend our broken hearts

Though our love is healing

We deserve a chance to love again.

In separate rooms, we cry alone

To wash away the hurt we both feel.

We gave love a chance to breathe again.

Our hearts was full of pain, and hard to forgive

The only thing I feel and see, were you?

I never thought it would come to this.

Divorce

1 John 1:1-10

1) That which was from the beginning, which we have heard, which we have seen with our eyes, which we have looked upon, and our hands have overseen, of the Word of Life.

2) For the life was manifested, and we have seen it, and bear witness, and shew unto you that eternal life, which was with the father and was manifested unto us.

3) That which we have seen and heard declare us unto you, that ye also may have fellowship with us: and truly our fellowship is with the Father, and with his Son Jesus Christ.

4) And these things write us unto you, that your joy may be full.

5) This then is the message which we have heard of him, and declare unto you, that God is light, and in him is no darkness at all.

6) If we say that we have fellowship with him and walk in darkness, we lie and do not the truth:

7) But if we walk in the light, as he is in the light, we have fellowship one with another, and the blood of Jesus Christ his Son cleanseth us from all sin.

8) If we say that we have no sin, we deceive ourselves, and the truth is not in us.

9) If we confess our sins, he is faithful and just to forgive us our sins and to cleanse us from all unrighteousness.

10) If we say that we have not sinned, we make him a liar, and his word is not in us.

Deep in a silent nighttime, carve out space into everlasting time. I spoke for forgiveness, and it spoke back with you are forgiveness. I walked in trumpet that moment in time that I carve out of space, and within that moment of time, I was born. I open my eyes to see the sun, moon from heaven, hollowing out hills and rivers where I stood before time itself begin. My heart was filled with laughter, and He told me everything was going to be all right just hold on to my unchanging hand.

I was amazed and overwhelm at the beauty of my Lord and the creator juices that flowed. I will be there for you, and I will abide with thee through it all, He said. I will stand by your during your troubles, problems and all that linger to harm you. Through your trials and tribulations, I will be your arm bearer, your knight in shining armor that will fight your battles now and those that are yet to come. I have you back hence fort and forever more, for you are my creation.

Chapter 1
God compassion and our Fears

Roman 3: 23 For all have sinned and come short of the glory of God.

24. Being justified freely by his grace through the redemption that is in Christ Jesus

"God had giving you the freedom to listen to yourself."

"Divorce is not your misfortune just another avenue for the Lord to bless you through."

Not everyone is willing to admit that their marriage was a joke from the beginning and their marriage was like a nightmare taking place on Jason Street. The greatest stage in life is create by individuals who are promise to each other but are still waiting on the stage for its greatest performance to act out their true love but never understanding the clue when to start acting/action.

Any marriage at any giving time can blast into orbit, and the fall back to reality can be a great fall. One of the sadly and most frustrating experience of anyone personally life is dealing with an ex-spouse who little and profound thoughts have left them fighting with the turmoil of life that has made them feel worthless.

When a spouse is unwilling to change or admit to their part in a fragile marriage, it can cause the marriage to fall under the curse of sin and the rules that governed it. Therefore, under the curtains of feeling and emotions fear is born as ruler of the nest. Fear cut down and cut into the adulthood of a man and, at the same time, cut-away the figment of woman's love that would normally sustain a man's ability to love her. If the keel of love is never measured, either party will never know the depth of each other love for one another love. Open wounds will parallel the floodgate of uncertainty that will corrupt the very root of the marriage through disbandment that is subject to fear itself.

A spouse can feel and see the fear in their partner eyes, but at the same time can hold the marriage together and their dreams if they continue to believe in each other. They can overcome if they put forth the effort to seek the truth in the marriage that wills strengthen it. The process of fear starts the moment we reject the idea that love is not anymore and there is nothing to hold on to or fight for. Sin will penetrate the wholeness of the marriage where love resides by placing love in a non-value state. Fear is a micro-opened that controls the gateway to the heart that, blocked out reality and blinds the input that stimulates the marriage from being fruitful. Fear existence between space and time that takes up matter within the cell wall of love and hate. The walls of the heart pushes hurt and pain to create moment of abnormal behavior that will open doors for other opportunities to self-create in an unhealthy relationship by manifesting itself throughout the marriage.

Fear can be mid-life crises, losing what you have not understanding what you need and want in life. Fears can come from anywhere at any given time by way of hurt and disappointment. Not knowing where to look and take the right step can push a marriage in the wrong direction and, in most cases, create a battlefield between couples that can last for years to come? Not knowing the Lord for yourself or having a shoulder to lean on or a source you can depend on can leave a marriage feeling hopeless and uncoordinated.

Fear come from words that are spoken, and our heart is not receiving very well. Our spouse spoken words can be thought provoking and can flow from our lips with ease. This can leave the marriage in a cripple state of being. To push through this, you must get control of thoughts and put fewer negative reactions into place that you will live to regret. So, in other words, watch what you say and how you say it to your spouse, they are the ones you must live with and come home to and see every day.

As communication between spouses become non-existence on each level. They start to feel uncomfortable and insecure in the marriage. False marriages create misunderstanding that goes out the window and fall on the ground of deaf ears. When if it returns, and it will return as a mad dog out of control and will look like your past with great hate and come with revenge that will remind you every day what you did wrong but never able to explain or tell you why. When couple failure to open and dialogue about issues that are affecting their marriage, they will find themselves walking on the cord of destruction with their back against the wall.

Things could be better or run smoother if "Both" hearts, souls, and minds were on the same page. As your spouse voice echoes through your heart like a hollowing wolf, and the places where you feel frighten and bitten keep opening like never ending dripping fault. These experiences never seem to heal or never find an opportunity to heal, which will leave you frustrated and irritated. There are voices that will cut deep into your well-being as if you were prey just been caught in snare. A game of disrespect from both parties can have everlasting effect, and person with disabilities each one's ability to take control of a situation by overpowering the standard of love. But the love of the Lord is so compassionate that he can feel you touching the hem of his garment.

The Lord had a compassionate heart that can reach over and beyond our understanding into our worse time and redeem us from it all. The Lord sees the positive in his creature, but we bring out the worse in everyone that we encounter and come across in a negative. This behavior has an everlasting effect on your development and future service with the Lord. To do the will of the Lord you must be willing to change your present situation and walk in a new direction. People in and out of the church hold different point of views about how God blessed them and others.

Just because you know the Lord one way and, but your spouse is acting like they never knew the Lord. There is no need to feel disconnected or lacking in your ability to serve the Lord with an open heart. The Lord does not want you to fall from heaven; he just wants to bless you. It's normal Saint's like us to go to church and pray every day, then turn around and make a mistake about our situation. We go to church to rebuild our relationship with the Lord, but we must be willing to seek help to rebuild our marriage as well with our ex's. We must be willing to forgive and move forward in the word of the Lord with understanding that we all have come short of his glory and must repent for our sinful ways.

There are couples who refused to forgive their spouse by keeping old mess alive and well in the marriage. They never figure it out, if they forgive their spouse for his or her wrongdoing, the Lord will show them mercy and grace, but they never come to that conclusion, so they are never off the hook. So, they keep applying the pressure to the wound(s) that never find time to heal. So, you will spend the rest of your life with this person walking around as a wounded soul. (As the old saying goes, no one want you when you are down and out).

One of the worse mistake couples can make in life and during their transformation into their marriage is they stop praying and believing in one another. They leave the Lord out of each movement in the marriage by making excuses that they can oversee life's little difficulties themselves. While this attitude gone uncheck, small debris turn into large emptiness spots that is never filled with anything but garbage or leftover from previous relationship/marriage. Because everything that you are doing is never check in the Lord therefore life becomes worthless. God is not about condemning separation that led to your divorce but about building marriage where separation never can take root to live.

Conflict comes about when we start to listen to others and their point of views, which sway our way of thinking. We stop listening to the Lord and start listening and depending on our own understanding. Just because your friend(s) had option about something does not mean you have to make it your option. We start judging others they live and what they have and less by the content of their character. We get out of harmony with the Lord as we begin to self-medicine ourselves, and conflict grows from that unreliable source. If our heart is not filled with the love of God, we are subject to step over the line at any given time into a prodigy lifestyle. Who can we blame when we are not showing God true love of compassion to others?

When we are doing our own thing, we do not think about the outcome down the road. We produce excuses because our life is so right, and others are living so wrong. We never think about the consequences of our own action, just the acts of others. We kept pointing fingers at each other for our shortfalls. (Roman 18:12) tell us that we should be at peace with each other and live in harmony with one another. I believed that, but the problem with that is our ability to let go of the past and live with our decisions. To disagree with our past is not to depend on it for our understanding but experience. Also, we are to learn from our mistakes and put the past behind us, build on your experiences through the Lord, Jesus Christ, who strengthens us daily.

If it is not possible to have face-to-face talk with someone who had cause us great conflict or causes great harm in our life, it might be possible to sit down and write them a letter. A letter for discontentment and disappointment might do the job. Finding the right moment to put your thoughts on paper and address your concerns is one way of getting our point across. Some say there is nothing wrong with drinking it when you get drunk that makes all the difference. You see your attitude about thing change because they get out of focus.

Where did it all go wrong and why it happen, and how did this happen is a mystery for some and a clear answer for other's when sin is behind it all. You must be willing to open yourself up to the possibility that your thoughts will be rejected and overlooked the importance of life. If you allow, you are flesh to rule, then you will have no voice. When you have done all that you can do, you have done your part when a face-to-face is not possible, and the victim of the offense is unwilling to meet your half-way, just maybe a letter will do the job.

Face-to-face, in some cases, are not good for reconciliations until the air is cleared and you feel your heart can communicate on a God giving purpose. Sometimes we cannot light our furnace because we are too far into ourselves, and we only see the fault in others. Receiving hurt and pain behind foolishness is unfair, so you can say what. Sometime, the hurt and pain is more than skin deep; it rattled the soul and places you in dreadful position. ("Roman 12:18, where Paul speaks about living peaceably with all individuals"). So, I ask you, why pull yourself in the hands of the enemies when they do not want to live in peace with you.

(Wisdom tell us: if a person does not want you, they just do not want you and will give an Oscar performance to show it)

I never understood hurtful words until I asked my ex to what extent did, I hurt her so bad for her to treat me so closed mind and treat me so bad. Words from your spouse can cut to the bone. When a spouse simple word said, **I never wanted you,** I wanted someone else. You can hold on to those hurtful words for many years until you start to hurt in places you never thought was possible, or I did not know the Do can hurt so bad, but it did. I thought I was prepared for anything, but those words left me with an empty feeling that my life was melting away (like a block of ice thrown in a furnace). I almost gave up, but the Lord in me refused to let me fall by the wayside. That old saying is not true that sticks and stones might break my bones, but words will never hurt you, they lied to you and me. They forget to tell us that they were living on an isolated island in the middle of nowhere, or never been married, or never experience love at all.

I pray sometime: My prayer Lord, My Lord, my Lord, my Lord, I knowth thy have been good to me. You had sprung from the depth of my soul with the spring of tomorrow, given me living hope. You gave me the vision that today is the day that my spouse will understand that I hurt, to. Lord, I know that your words are true. For my life have changed and never been the same since you came into my life. You had been there for me from the beginning of my crises and through my uncertainly. I have searched the world over and all I found was unrest. Lord, you have giving me a shoulder to lean on and understanding that you will see me through. You have showed men love and showered me with love. Furthermore, I appreciated your presence in my life. Yet, I fail before you, Lord, and you still saw fit to save a sinner like me. My marriage failed, I had to start over and the moment I cried alone, and I thought you were not here for me, how wrong was I to think that way of you? You were there for me every step of the way. Forgive me, O' Lord, I was trying to make things right without your guidance, and you saw fix to help, and I thank you. Amen!

(P-S)! My Lord, I wrestle with the unknowns that is trying to empower themselves through my misfortunate. I've trying to grow and face my insecurities that are holding me back that had caused me to not believe in myself. I fear things in my past that is haunting me and causing me to lose sight of my goal. But without you, I would just simples pass away and one day awaked forever lost in time. Lord your compassion is time and time updated back and forth. I am here because of you; you have allowed me to experience life in triumph. I just only want to say thank you for my life. You are my living water that quenches my burning thirst. You are my living bread, my mantle from heaven all that I will ever need. Lord, you spoke life into my situation and from that, my spirit grew from your words that supplied me with living substance.

Lord, I have meditated upon my mission that you have entrusted me with, and I am willing to run this race to the end. You stepped into my life with changes and saved a sinner like me who was struggling to hold on to and maintained the faith. Lord, your love is compassion, and your kindness is overwhelming that sinner like me who now have the right to the Tree of Life is graceful and merciful to be counted in that number. Lord, as your love unfolds before me, my weak spot growing, and I was strengthening by the love of your eyes watching upon me. Now, I look back in time and see with ease the blessing of your love flowing around and through me.

Lord, your warm and kind spirit embraced me and transformed me anew. I can step out with ensured that you are there for me. I am so thankful that you saw something in a sinner like me that was worth saving. Lord, you have increased my daily bread and gave me a daily walk that I can talk in the comfort of your strength. I have experienced you and I know you have blessed me in ways I can only fall on my knees and be thankful that you saw something in me. Lord, as my thoughts each day are more of you and the more I speak of you and represent you I can face the world as it turns and move from my edge of night into the marvelous light.

"Holy Spirit will beep when the conscious is turned off."

The Lord is a Keeper

Isaiah 1:18

("Come now, and let us reason together, saith the Lord: though your sins be as scarlet, they shall be as white as snow; though they be red like crimson, they shall be as wool").

The word of the Lord was also stated in ("St John 3: 16 that "God so loved the world, that he gave his only begotten Son. That whoever believeth in him should not perish but have everlasting life"). Our need for peace escapes us sometimes. As we wrestled with the thoughts of our past, we fill with guilt. Our clouded mind becomes unclear, and our unsettled past is like a storm that never seems to go away or calm down... Before we find total commitment again, we beat ourselves up and over repeatedly behind foolish thinking and reaction that is relating to our past decisions.

But I bestow upon you the word of the Lord that stated that he will never forsake us or leave us. In the word of our Lord alone, he thought about us in our time of need. He knew disappointing days like this could come that we will need him by our side. When loyalty, reliability, trustworthiness is lost, and you feel alone, and you have no one you can call on and depend on. The Lord will be there for us to hold us and see us through our turmoil.

He gave himself not only to live among men, to bear our sins, and die as a sacrifice all lamb but to be our keeper. Your need for peace is a standard before the Lord, and within him is the plea for mercy and grace. Christ identifies with our sufferings and understands our needs for humanity. He is one with God who has linked himself with the children of humankind by ties a notch in our life that can never be broken. Jesus is not ashamed to call you sibling or family, but we need to turn from our wicked ways and embrace the knowledge of the Lord by repenting.

He will welcome us back into the fold and give us a new lease on life. As he welcomes us back into his kingdom, we no longer will he capsize or shipwreck in the worse time of our life. We can come ashore with the grace of the Lord being our witness. We have a lifeline that will bring us to shore and be our life source. ("In Hebrews 2:11 He tell us that he will be our Sacrifice, our Advocate, our brother, and our sister bearing our human form before the Father's throne and through eternal grace mending us from the sin of time"). He did this that we might be uplifted from the ruin and degradation of sin, that we might reflect the love of his Father and share the joy of holiness.

The price that he paid for us is a notable example of God's love for us and the willing to forgive us of our sins. His exalted conceptions of what we may become through Christ, who strengthen us and welcome us into his fold, is a standard that we can bring into the fold of love by forgiving other for their shortfalls. The more I study the divine love of God, the more I am inclined to understand the battle that fought at the cross and victory that gave the right to pardon from our sins. The characters of God love ring from heaven like the windows of heaven opening and pouring out its blessing. Through my divorce, I have learn more about his mercy, tenderness, and forgiveness blended with equity and justice and, more clearly, the love of God in me.

His innumerable evidence of love that is infinite and transferred to us stand to this day, and there is no need for me to give that up and die in sin knowing what I know now. The Lord power is a work in progress that is working from the inside to change me and my way of thinking. Before our life can be changed, we must understand the source in which outside forces are acting to get a reaction. A new life from Christ above can open the door to full healing and remove sin in our life. His grace alone can quicken the lifeless faculties of the soul and attract it to God to holiness once again. ("John 3:3 tells us unless a man is born again, he can't see the kingdom of God").

Love and giving back walk together.

Forever Loving the Lord

Let us not love with words or tongue but with actions and in truth.

(1 John 3:18)

Lord, you know you blessed me.

I know, you know.

You gave me heaven on earth.

Like the sizzling sun, you made

That sits heavenly above.

So, my love for you still beats in my heart.

As the days of my life grow old

Your precious love ring like a heavenly bell

That I so gently touch to feel your presence

Like an earthly phone dialing in

O'Lord, you know how you bless me.

You kept me warm when the nights were cold.

My body, mind, and soul you hold.

Everyday Lord, during my wounds

I thank you for my healing.

From your gift, I grasp the true meaning of your love

Like looking into heaven from an open widow

I see your smile inside of happiness all roll in one.

I spend endless hours feeling close to thee.

On a frosty winter night, my body longs for the chill of fire

A breeze that kept my soul warm in middle of the summer

Not to freeze, not to get too hot.

My love for you formed an everlasting bond.

That I cannot live or do without

I speak to you, my Lord, with love, like never ending time.

You are my everlasting branch that I lean on

My beloved cornerstone I stand on.

I see my savior in shining armor riding up.

Across the open sky to heal my wounds

Let me speak to thee with my love,

My Lord, with words so sweet you gave me.

My voice, my heart, I will praise and lift thee.

You are not a Lord that's

I am afraid to show my love to

You knew my heart would hurt.

You knew I would need your support.

You knew I would cry,

You knew I would need someone.

To wipe the tears from my eyes

You knew my heart would bleed.

So, you gave me a special healing.

Now I understand something clearly at last.

In my hurt,

You knew my pain would cause my heart to ache.

You knew my heart would need healing again.

You knew I would not keep silent once you blessed me.

That my silence would be my cry

That the understanding you gave me would enlighten me

That your love is my connection

You knew the day would come.

I would need strong arm to hold me.

I would need a shoulder to support me through my afflictions.

I need pillow to lay my weary head; when my eyes are heavy.

You knew the day my divorce would be final.

And my pain would set in, and my heart would be heavy.

You knew my road to recovery would be long and tiresome,

But you showered me with love for you knew.

I would forever love the Lord.

Commitment of Love

First Peter 4:8

This passage tells us, "Above all, love each other deeply, because love covers over a multitude of sins."

Loving each other deeply opens wounds and hurtful that will begin to heal. As Our love because our covenant for each other shortfalls, we begin to experience forgivingness and give courage a push forward into our future. Commitment comes through deep prayers that are a love gift that is wrapping around the heart. Commitment of love refreshed itself by focusing on being in-love with the one who loves you with all thy heart, soul, and mind. Forgiveness is one method that love abides by. Love and understanding are a standard that we all live by. Love seeks to understand the importance of becoming as one and applied those rules to the heart. Love submits and sometimes stands alone and feels isolated and unconditional. The items that stand the test of time are mercy, kindness, and love. Love being the of them all is worth the causes. The Love that matched love is the love for God and others, then self.

You see, God is divine and everlasting, and your ways are not his ways. Therefore, the ties to sin can unlink you or separate you from the blessing of Christ. In your own way of thinking, sin can push you over the edge. As the pouring rain in the middle of a dry heat wraps itself around the very essence of your life, sin can evaporate your love for God and place evil before your eyes. Love says love them that love you, therefore, love abides with you and grace of your heart is never ending but should be always forgiving. Therefore, God is the source of your life and sustainer of your well-being that, equal to the commitment of love.

FOOTSTEPS OF LOVE

Psalm 17:5-6

5. My steps have held to your paths; my feet have not slipped.

6. I call on you, O God, for you will answer me; give ear to me and hear my prayer.

Psalm 119:133

Direct my footsteps according to your word; let no sin rule over me.

I heard footsteps in time of despair.

Like shadows playing in the dark

Soft words spoke, springing from his lips.

He is stepping across time and space into my presence.

He came with love that forgave my past.

Footsteps with a voice so soft

With love that flashed with keys

To unlock my heart to love again.

Like visions and imagines, he painted a picture

Like angles dancing in heaven

Hanging out on the clouds,

Playing Ping-Pong with the stars

Footsteps of love he showered me.

We spoke openly and honestly about my pain.

With gifts and words, he encouraged me.

There is no reason to fear my love is pure.

Trials, tribulations, and divorce might come.

But my love for you will abide.

I will never step back or leave you dinging.

My spirit is never diminishing.

My eyes will always behold you.

I will answer your calls like time itself.

Giving inspirational words not to worry

For I will comfort you from this point on

For you are the soul I hung and died for

On Calvary, I pleaded your case

I gave your life purpose and meaning.

You can stop struggling, you have my love.

With that, you can fully serve your purpose

All the time, you spoke wildly.

I love you unconditionally.

Not only with words

But with all my heart, soul, and mind

I still believe in you; I will never divorce you.

For you are my footsteps of love across time

A LOVE THAT IS REAL.

John 15:9-11

⁹ As the father has loved me, so have I loved you? Now remain in my love. ¹⁰ If you keep my commands, you will remain in my love, just as I have kept my father's commands and remain in his love. ¹¹ I have told you this so that my joy may be in you and that your joy may be complete.

1 John 4: 10-12

¹⁰ This is love: not that we loved God, but that he loved us and sent his Son as an atoning sacrifice for our sins.¹¹ Dear friends, since God so loved us, we also ought to love one another. ¹² No one has ever seen God; but if we love one another, God lives in us, and his love is made complete in us.

I planted a seed, looking for harvests in you. I gave until it hurt, but my eyes were set on tomorrow, you know, by how that turned out. My heart moves in patterns that were ungodliness like a kiss or hug that make me feel like a thief in the night. As the blood passes through every portion of the body, you feel an emotional tie that taught us what love feel like or should be like. What we feel and come to know gave us what we need to overcome and become the eighth wonder of the world in love by our rights.

By building tears of restrict, we become unholy and ungodliness because we hid behind and refused to surrender to what we know is the right thing to do. Our unconscious does notbe afraid of darkness but does understand the true meaning of touch and what it takes to commit to its true feeling. In this step, our word becomes a link that bind us to darkness and from that darkness flowed the issue of our imagination. We get lose during our trials and tribulations by putting ourselves first, and the Lord last.

Because we do not understand the desire to please the Lord, we translate unhealthy habits into insecurity feels our infected attitude begin to play tricks on our mind. Our daily walk is unparallel and divided into part that cannot be recognized until we put the Lord first in our life and move with grace and forgiveness through repentance. By this time, our heart will suffer the consequences of slowly dying without Christ in your life. If we fail to remove ourselves from the very thing that causes us great suffering and causing us to face hardship's, things in our life will get out of control and causes us to live a rough and rugged life.

In our lives, we play the role of hurt without pain, but that is impossible to do with our current situation. We will face the trumpet that will play the song to start our march on judgment day. Our social members and function parts will dry up and slowly disappear before our very eyes because we walk in darkness with our eyes closed to the possibilities that the Lord can and will to be our light from and through darkness.

Sometimes, we need additional information to hurdle over our hills in our life that we take for granted. We live with steppingstones and with bottle neck lives that we sometimes cannot face or produce a suitable solution that will give us the tools that will enlighten our journey. Blind spots in our life can in most cases, cause us to go through things that we normally would not face or come across. But that is the way life is when it come to moving around with the face of darkness as our guide. This movement will not allow us to see over or around our present situation if we are walking and associate with gloominess. We put ourselves in offensive positions that bring tears from our heart.

We try to ease back into our comfort zone only to discover that we have nowhere to hide. Our heart will tell off on us. As our present situation presents itself, our unknown moves into the farther state of our mind only to stay alive and move throughout and roundabout our daily living. Our heart ends up sometimes in an unpleasant situation, and prayers and presence of the Lord is the only answer that will see us through. Sometimes, we fail to see the handwriting on the wall, so we walk around blind to the fact that we are looking in the wrong direction for comfort. This emotion and bad feeling can, in most cases, gives us a bad result. We seek simple answers but sometime only to find that the small detail of our decision will be displayed across the face of resentment.

It is at this time that we become our worse enemies like dry bones in the valley our goals and abilities are never realizes because we never find any corrected method to help us move forward in a positive direction. There are stages or levels in our life that once we experience hardship or discomfort, we have tension to move in negative direction that will start to corrupt the very fiber of our beings. We need to turn from our wicked way seek out the Lord in our life. As our heart address the fundamental function of the human anatomy.

It is clear in others mind that our weakness is our downfall as if they have never made a mistake. The presence of the Lord in our life can be helpful and healthy. Our heart searched out the passion and mercy in love that can relate to others that is feeling our pain. There are issues that humanity must face to live life to the fullest. The mere facts that life offers little or no boundary for others hurtful attitude toward us this one reason sin should be put away and not dealt with no means. But as human, this gives us the right to understand and move in a positive direction away from the hurt and pain that once controlled our life and living.

There is heaven and a hell, and it is your choice to choose. Life does exist and leaves small room for marginal error and no second chance to live life again in the form as we know it. As spouses searched their heart to unravel the hurt and unkindness of one another, it is understood that most individualsdo not live like you do or want to. They have no desire to wake up one day in heaven because all they know is hell.

These issues crossed all boundaries and barrel of communication base upon the ground the Christ do live in us and maintain resident in the moral of our soul. But, some couples refused to recognize those boundaries or barrel of communication by moving into their own form of understanding. The heart, soul and mind cannot be overlooked in a marriage but must be dealt with in the most humanitarian way. Many have overlooked the true facts about Christ and foundation that he stands on and did for us has brought us this far and closer to heaven. So where do you stand with Christ in your life as you search through the mass of confusion and dismal surrounding you. Sometimes, you can be overwhelming and heartbreaking to a point that it will leave you grasping for air.

The commitment of love focuses on being in love with the one you love. Forgiveness is one method that love abides by. Love and understanding are standards that we all should live by. Love seeks to understand the importance of come as one and applied the rules to the heart. In most cases, love stand alone with unconditional love to hold hands with forgiveness to rescue your soul from the abyss. The items that stood the test of time are Mercy, kindness, and love. The greatest of them all is love, your love for God and others, then self. You see, God is divine and everlasting, and your ways are not his ways. Therefore, the tires of sin can be linked to pouring rain in the middle of your life. Love says that I love you because you love me; therefore, love abide with you, and grace of your heart, and love is never ending.

An Oil Painting of Love

[10] This is love: not that we loved God, but that he loved us and sent his Son as an atoning sacrifice for our sins. [11] Dear friends, since God so loved us, we also ought to love one another. [12] No one has ever seen God; but if we love one another, God lives in us, and his love is made complete in us.

Oil painting of my life was not painted by the expert's hands of my life. I was left out in the cold, and I had a picture of me to look at. I believe in what you see is what you get, and I held fast to that. I never looked deep at the surface of love, and I never wondered at what length love would go to pull you back into the folder and love you the same as yesterday. My heart was a picture of what love should look like and what I wanted love to be and feel like.

Never understanding the full scope of your own heart and how it has affected you and what level you are on should never be a struggle, but it was for a divorcee like me. As I raced across the abyss of times, I begin to recall momentous events that led up to this moment. The effect of time and my time did not coincide with the work that was yet to be done. A portrait of my life flashed before me like time itself. As my life was unleashing, the very thing that I had been running from was finally caught up with me.

The emotion of darkness was trying to pull me back into the old ways of living. But I look back at my blessings and what the Lord had did for me. I said no to what sin was offering and felt good about my decision. There were moments I lost my focus by looking for love in the wrong places. I learned love come by way of the heart through sight of knowing what you want and need in your life, which will complete you. I could see where sin had reduced me to nothing.

My life was being pushed in the wrong direction. My life was no more than a steppingstone into hell, where sin started to burn out of control like wildfire. I was going down for the last count, but I believed in the Lord and all that he could do for me. My life had shifted into chaos and slowly being corrupt by falling debris that was clamping onto my soul. As I stood back and observed the color lines of my demising life, I was shocked at the result I was faced with.

A beautiful feeling came over me, and I knew at that moment a better day would come, and I will be to overcome them through Christ who strengthens me. I was captured and overwhelmed by this, so I cried. Early involvement with sin came with a price to this day, I am still struggling with and fighting against. They said freedom come with a price how well do I understand that. I am looking forward to the moment in time that I am free from the very natural of sin.

Sometime the price of sin comes with an over the limit sticker. You had a fervent desire and overwhelming desires to continue with the pro and con of sinning. Sin can, in most cases, designs and developed your life and push you to your outer limit. How my life would have turn out without the Lord, only the God known. What now I do know my life without God would be empty and void without him, I would just simply existence without purpose and aimless moving about. I saw my selfish ways flashing before me like a mighty rushing wind. The smallest and unimportant thing in my life seems to upset me the most, and I would find myself struggling just to hold on.

Hundreds of paintings, watercolors, and pastels trace the evolution of my life, forming the mid-eighty's and outward, exploring the various stylistic and thematic phases of my life to the point of little value now that my heart was missing the most important thing that have been keeping it alive. My work continues throughout my young days to conquer the old fears that show a long and rich tradition of realism. My own colorfully modern style combines with abstraction became serious to me that I was willing to give up everything to be a winner, no matter what it took. As my past drew closer to me, the canvas of my life draws a picture that was unforgettable. My blood oozed with a burning desire to know more why divorce hurt so badly, and the struggle was endless.

The clock on the city sky tower read 3:26 am. The light on the left of me and the dark highway to the right of me reflected in my eyes, where the head beam light reflected across space and time. The green grass was gray in the background of the night as city lights forced themselves upon the night. As lifelines divided the left and the right side of my life, I saw pictures of yesterday and all my hurts and pains healing. The good and bad were going and coming in both directions, that suffering appeared to be normal and out of control at the same time. Hedges on both sides of my life gave me a feeling that I was not alone. As arrows of life pointed to the left and right of my life, trouble were pushing me in all the wrong directions. As discoloration of life reflected upon the image of my trials and tribulations, I was moved and sadden to think I had come this far only to experience another letdown.

As the morning unfolded and hours washed away like sand on the beach, as tears streamed from my eyes, I thought how blessed I was. A density of hope came into sight as a quick rush, and I pushed forward to conquer my fears. I could see a shadowing body still moving about the dark sky in my mind. It was yesterday that I was thinking hard about as the background canvas appeared next to a blue line of nature as waggled edges of space. Mountains grew in height and depth as I turned the corner and made my way back from yesterday thoughts and hurtfulness. I watched the flashers of my life as the distance light came into focus and push my mind back into reality.

One spot of my life would not speak to me, and I was trying to run away from all the pain I was feeling now. I was unable to change the color within the background of my life because that part of my life was my past. And straight from the heart, I could not sleep or find a resting place to lay my weary head. While other parts of my life were mapped and appeared to be greenish in color with a dash of hope.

While dark green and off-white with a strike of blue and strip of brown, as the wind blew my life back and forth in the dark in my life like a ray of hope uncoordinated with the rising of the morning sun that was sucking up the morning dew. As my eyes viewed the towel, my status, I could not help but to notice the colors that was ripping across the open sky, glittering off the night-light to give open to a dark-orange color in the biological lights of my life.

Love step into my heart and open a new view that appeared within the eyesight my beloved heart. Blue strikes run down and across the centerpiece of the heart. I could feel the pain of yesterday. My dying pain was seeking desire to park my heart on a parallel line that would chase down the open sky and beg for its forgiveness.

The chambers of at the bottom quarter of my heart looped around and over onto the canvas that covered my heart with a logo in the middle of it, stamped pain and difficulty. Each door of the heart open to the highway of regrets that was like hinging hanging on by a spider web in the corner of your web of lies. As the vessels of my love extended their arms across pain into an open mask of screaming turmoil that led to floodgates of my emotions that was hanging on to yesterday's painful thoughts and disappointments.

Yesterday arm painted a picture that ran the full length of my heart, leaving me with the impression that life and living does not existence. As my life's experience stop and go, there were times I was going to make it. Sometime, my pain appeared to have stopped for a period, and other times, it was part halfway across the highway of life waiting for a jumpstart to start over. The side curve of my life was leaving inward, not outward, as thought unfolded before drained mind with little or no remorse. As sin leaped off the page from the night light into my lap, I could feel the pressure of sin's presence coming alive in my life to remind me I had not made it yet.

Images ranging from half the distance to a flat bottom of hope that you could feel like a tornado coming out of nowhere to rip you apart and toss you to the wind of sins. Sin's eyes looked over at me with certain hatred, as if sin were reading my mind. All the lights of my life came on. As the shadows of grays, blues, yellows flashing through my window shield as the morning dew blinded me. Suddenly, I understood what the Lord was trying to show me and what love was trying to say and do. The Lord point-of-view of love was clear and motion that rekindled my heart to forgive and love after my divorce, for I knew the Lord has love me through all my trials and tribulations, for my heart lives.

CHAPTER 2
Loving and Sharing

1 John 4:10-12

10. Herein is love, not that we loved God, but that he loved us and sent his Son to be the propitiation for our sins.11. Beloved if God so loved us, we ought also to love one another.

12. No man hath seen God at any time. If we love one another, God dwelleth in us, and his love is perfected in us.

Loving and sharing mean having someone that you can enjoy and reap the benefits of having that person being in your life. Love and sharing boiled down to how you treat the relationship and your spouse. When couples fail to understand the touch of God's love it is difficult to spread love or share love with someone else. By understanding your responsibility and God's position in your life and your purpose will grow outside the four walls of your normal daily walk with Christ. You can begin to grasp the full effect of divine Love. Loving and sharing is growing actions that encourage, enhance, embrace, empower the relationship to move and keep moving in a spiritual way that allowed the Lord to be your solid rock.

Sharing during challenging times help love to move in a positive direction by during the right thing that stimulate love to move in a positive direction that will increase your relationship with your spouse and Christ. When a fire is slowly burning out, there is still a glimpse of hope left in a spark that will start the fire over. That sparker is Christ, who is waiting patiently on you. These principles, or the mustard seed effect, keep the home fire burning. All marriages should focus on Jesus Christ as the main source of existence and the center of their life. The home fire will keep burning and burn away any impurity that might cause you to slip and fall away from your blessings. Therefore, you can stand on a solid rock and see the foundation of love beneath you that supported your every move through life trials and tribulations. Love can be the wind beneath your wing that will allow you to see farther into the future.

When love is feeling you and returned through the blessing of Christ will be your spouse bridge across trouble water and enshrine their heart with understanding that they will be there for you. Like sweet fragrance, the Lord love cannot be hidden. On the cross, he died for you and I and to this day, He still stand in the mist of your troubles for you. As you meet others, his love will spread and move in an encouraging way that will help you grow in strength and vision of the Lord. When the Lord become the source of your life and, you can move like a spring in the desert that bring fort refreshing water from a dry well. And those who are eager to drink from the cup of life will find themselves as a source in life that the Lord can use as they fight their uphill battles.

As you move into different stage of God love, his love will be manifested as a desire to work in your favor to bring you from you past to a more harmony present. ("Matthew 20:28 states that: The Son of man came not to be ministered unto, but to minister, and to give His life a ransom for many.") The sooner the Lord comes into your life, your world will be your world turn, and no more searching for tomorrow at the edge of night for the Lord will be your guiding light.

The things you used to do, you will do no more, for the Lord has brought you out of darkness into the marvelous light. There will come a time in your life that rebirth will take place, and your heart will desire to make known to others what a precious friend you have found in Jesus. How blessed you are now that the Lord is in your life and everything that you possess is happiness in your life, and the Lord will provide those moment that will last.

If sometime taste good to you and it feel good to you, it is hard to hold that in and not let it flow in your daily walk. Knowing that the joy someone has brought and saw you through will be ful filled, you deepen dream you are most likely to grow spiritually and in harmony with them. You want the world to know that there is something good about you that the Lord sees in you after your divorce that everyone had missed. For the Lord will show the world what they missed, and your spouse had walked away from and lost in the process of not knowing and tasting and seeing what it means to have a true and devoted relationship with Christ.

We need to cultivate a friendship in our life that will enrich our love for Christ and move us in right direction to fulfill our goals in Christ within our marriage by seeking the Lord first before we say I-Do. We should be able to tell the story how Christ changed our life and brought into the fold of his lovely care and develop our relationship in him through marriage. The activities that reflect upon our marriage and throughout the public should be produced that the universe should see the Lord working in us. We shall seek to be in the presence of the Lord by letting our work speak for us. The ability for Christ to take away our hurt and causes us to suffer less is nothing shorter than a blessing within itself and a plus in our life that we should give back to the Lord in praise.

"John 1:29 states that he will take away the sin of the world, and that include you and me." Christ sufferings on the cross allowed sinner to repent and move closer to the Lord away from their sinful nature. We are brought into sympathy and harmony with the Lord through fellowship. A reflection upon oneself will reflect upon their marriage and public notice to oneself. All blessing that flows with equal response from you is opportunity for God to bless the marriage as it fully blossom. At this point, God can use a marriage as it potential push to serve and grow within the region of God Holiness.

Blessing in a marriage is like having your cake and eating it to. The love that you give will reaction and develop longevity and everlasting relationship that upheld the principles of marriage within the constitution of the marriage, and it will show others how God plan for married should grow and develop. This is one of God purpose for a family or a single partner hood to grow in Christ. The plan can only work if it is clear and with understanding that couples must act and take part in God plan for salvation and believing that he is Lord of Lord and King of King. Therefore, married couples will have privilege of becoming partakes of the divine intimacy within the marriage in the name of Christ, and nothing is off limit as God intended it to be.

God see your marriage as a purpose within the rim of His committed to your marriage to him. He is willing to go the extra mile to see you through until the end. His message is clear even to the angels of gospel that your married is heaven connected. In his infinite love for your marriage, Christ gives us purpose and meaning that we can connect to and a source that we can depend on to sees us through our troubling times. We can overcome dislikes with his love and guidance in Jesus Christ, who strengthens us daily, but we must walk in faith. Lord what to share his blessing, his joy, his spiritual uplifting, which will result in an unselfish ministry that represent His true and divine love for one another through him.

But sometimes, we get sidetrack in our own selfish ways and think we have all the answer to all questions because we have been misused in one form or fashion. The spirit of unselfish labor of love speaks about your gift of depth and understanding how the Lord is willing to work in your favor. Christ love is loveliness to peace and happiness that is brought into our possessor. His love reached deep into corners of the heart and find that innermost feeling that can express the spiritual perception while producing a steady growth in faith under the rules of the marriage. In creating a full divine purpose in your marriage, God is willing to lift your marriage to new height. The mechanic of God love is diligent and faithful representative of him who toiled in the lowly walks of our life and give us the strength to see beyond our faults and give us the vision to live through and around to bring us forth from our disappointments of divorce.

You may not see it now, but the Lord is working in your favor in your marriage. With the Love of the Lord in your life and spirit, He is willing to perform life's humblest duties to stand and fight to the very end for the marriage that sometime still end in divorce. There are times in our life through the process of divorce we do not see what the Lord has bestowed upon us because we become blind to hurt and daily pain. Because we refused to see the Lord Love is for what it is, we end up fighting a losing battle because we did not turn it over to him.

Colossians 3:23 tell us that if the love of God is in the heart, it will be manifested in the life. As Christ lifted us in our present surrounding, our influence will elevate and bless his name. Therefore, the Lord loves to share the depth of his love and salvation with us. You need the Lord in your life, and sometime a good thing is hard to find, so when you find it, hold on to it.

If the Lord is not in your marriage, nothing will feel right, and everything will be wrong. This can last a lifetime if your life is feed by the wrong source of life or living the wrong lifestyle before Christ. Couple's need to realize that marriage is a blessing and highly favorite in the Lord because of their commitment to the marriage. Couple's may not see the Lord giving them influence over their enemies until they see their enemies removed. God want your marriage to move forward, working the Lord assigned duties and responsibilities for the marriage that will make it work. In his likeness, his love has brought together a fitting life that He can stand next to and be a blessing to. He will increase your unseasoned joy, and he will fill your thirst of love through forgiveness.

ACTIVE RELATIONSHIPS COME WITH DEVOTION AND WITH A PURPOSE.

Active ingredient of commitment: "is what your spouse sees in you and what you are makes out of yourself and what they see you becoming."

Mission in commitment: "is walking together in Christ by building a marriage that is worthy to be praise; that will incorporate the heart, soul and mind on a foundation that you are willing to go the extra mile for."

"Visions with commitment: "are visions with positive steps that create positive ideas with achievable goals that you see your marriage going in to achieve fellowship with one another as one."

"As you live out the mission of your marriage and vision start to unfold God will open up the windows of heaven and pour out blessings upon you."

Christ's C/G=Center of Gravity

Proverbs 11:1

"A false balance is abomination to the Lord: but a just weight is his delight."

"Always keep the Lord as the center piece in your relationship or marriage. He will always guide and order your steps."

Since Jesus is the center balance of life, we cannot live in separate corner of our mind and achieve heavenly goals. All believers in Christ should worship God in spirit and in truth. The Lord wants our life to be balanced against the wages of sin that we might be able to withstand the arrows of our enemies.

"The Lord doesn't want our lives to be wasteful and buried in a life cycle of despair The Lord doesn't want sin to control your life or kill your optimistic views of life's blessings. The Lord wants you to withstand the arrows of sin in all directions of your life.. The cross that God carried was the love that balanced our faith between heaven and hell. God love focuses on the closeness that He had developed with his son, that his transformation off the cross will not be in vain in our life and living.

From Adam and Eve sinful act to our present condition, we are missing and lacking control of our lives by living on the edge and during our wicked ways. God's love also examines the balance of separateness and togetherness in marriages that He mended the bridge between now and forever. One of the greatest aspects of closeness is the balance that individual feel and had for each other. On the cross God provided provision for humanity to see undying love through his eyes and from his point-of-view. In a healthy marriage, God defined time together and time spent apart as closeness because it defined independent loyalty to the marriage but at the same time allowed individual to be themselves or co-existence in a developing marriage.

There is comfortable level that the Lord is trying to get us to and see His fullness. This emotional closeness and emotional separateness will not allow other person to step into your space between you and Christ. In this stepping process, the Lord want you to see the flexibility of his love and how it can be beneficial to you. By understanding this method, marriage can adjust and changes in their roles and develop response to stress and crisis through Christ. There are positions and decisions in life that will leave you stung and overwhelm and causes us to overreact and not react at all. At the same time, God is teaching us how to balance our love for each other. You can deny all the evidence presented before you and come up empty handed based on stupidity, but the question remains who is blessing you.

Your course of action and beliefs will push you over the edge or completely off balance. If you stop believing, your eyes will burst into tears, and your heart will fill up with hurt and pain that will cause you to sit sideways on life's unbalanced beam. If you take your eyes off the sparrow, you are subject to come up short at the crossroad of life. The Lord was in-love with his creation and loves it with all his heart, soul, and mind, that he was committed to show his undying love for it.

I believed and prayed that my prayers are answer with prayers that tomorrow want to be the same for divorce person. Loving the Lord should be express in the form of happiness that reached outward into a joyful noise and shouting in praising the Lord. I know the Lord love me more than I love myself. I believe I can sit beneath the wing of the Lord and be blessed. If ones fell to understanding God's desire for them and the love He had for them, it would be a shame to keep living life as they know it. His love is simple and never can be replaced and duplicated. Your misalignment and miscalculated feels of marriage should never be an obstacle for others to fall over.

In all cases, we must understand the misfortunate that forced us to move in a negative direction while the Lord is trying to redirect our lives back to him in a positive way. We must have honor and be willing to open our heart and let the Lord balance us and use us in his service. Sometimes, we refused to let the blessings of the Lord Produce happiness in our life. We find ourselves swallowing hooks, line and sinker, applying for an open position in the devil's workshop. We must be willing to become a vessel for the Lord to use and be a shining example for all to see.

We must pray and ask the Lord to step into our situation. If we know our situation is getting out of hand, there is no reason we should not ask the Lord to intervene on our behalf. We know our unbalance act and unsaying condition it trying to govern our daily life; we should give up that walk. What we see others do and watch them fail at, we should not emulate so willing.

"If we don't open our eyes and visit the true in our heart, we will fall by the wayside and lean to our own understanding."

We need to embrace our own marriage as others before us did by weathering the storm of marriage by being a living example. We should display our true feelings or emotions that will help us grow and develop solid ground in marriage. The Lord is Lord, and we all need Jesus in our life to develop into a usable product. He sees the worse in us and the best in us as we struggle to balance our daily walk with him. The road we walk and the choice we make are evident and obvious that we are walking on the wrong side of the road sometime. If we keep falling and getting up, this should let us know there is a God out there that is willing to help us to overcome our pitfalls. It is by design, not by incident, that God supports marriage, and he will function as a balance between failure and achievement. False marriage under false pretend cannot be balanced because they create their own world to live in and leave God out of it.

There is a need for the Lord to be in your life and move you in a direction that your marriage will represent him. You should not let anything separate you and your marriage from the blessing of the Lord. But sometimes, we stand on the outside of our marriage looking in and refuse to change the things that can make a different in our daily walk with Christ. So many times, we have failed at unimportant things and those unimportant things have turned into mountains that overwhelmed us. We cannot climb them or go through them or go around them, for we stand at the base of our mountain looking up with our hands folded. God cannot bless folded hands you need to lift them in praise.

Just to think, all the times you are wasted and not being productive has caught up with you. You have failed to reconnect, and by doing this, you never understood the fullness and the importance of comprehending the full score of God love. By doing this, you have left your family and yourself wide open for sin to come in and sit with you. It does not matter how low you are or how high you have reached. The format that we need to follow is Christ plan for our life and its driven purpose by being a living example that the Lord has set for couples to follow within the constitution of marriage. By refusing to let go and let the Lord use us we become puppets for the devil to mold.

Because of small thinking and not letting Christ be the center of gravity in our life, we suffer. Sometimes, it is not easy seeing how the Lord is going to bless us because we spend a percentage of our time looking the other way or over our shoulder; therefore, we get run over and knocked out in the process. In either direction, by moving in the Lord name, we can create a positive outcome and be blessed without any doubt. If you fall, you can get back up in the name of the Lord. When you are giving advice to others, let it be about where you been and what you did to overcome your dilemma. Draw a map in a way that closed eyes can see and a broken heart can mend, and in the presence of anyone that hear, you can be a witness to and feel the presence of the Lord in you.

If your life is balance correctly, Christ will always be your center of balance. The center of balance comes in three phases: Load, Freight and Burden. The weight of sin is the weight that stem from the load and the freight that you are carrying daily. Load is what you are carrying as a carrier and Freight is the past, present experiences are attached to each piece that is carried. The totally weight of sin is the most you can carry at any given time or your maximum storage capacity. Calculating life troubles and the movement that sin played will bring about a distribution of weight that positioned itself in your life to control your life. Each piece has its own weight that will bear down on you.

Phases of sin in a marriage are link together by a common cause. Each emotion and experience have a linking factor that act like and looks like the marriage that you were once in or a relationship that you once had. In most cases, silly games that sin play bring about a change in your life and bring out similar emotions and unstable behavioral in life cycle. As each incident begins to look like the past and as the past create fear factors that focus on your lack of Christ in your life, you will begin to overreact and produce chaos in your life.

It is at this point that trouble creeps into your life and move about your life with ease. As each act begin to mirror a broken marriage that masquerade itself as something good but gave you false hope that you can do things yourself and for yourself alone. When your past is surrounded by forgiveness, and your circumstances begin to act like or look like a previous relationship/marriage therefore, false hope is found, and you will find fault in your present condition. Some marriages refuse to move in a positive direction because they do not want to face the fact they must give up the wrong for the right.

Other words, they refuse because they must ask forgiveness and apologize for their wrongdoing and, in some cases, admit being partaker in the crime. A healing situation can present itself, if the marriage is open for suggestion to be used by the Lord.

Misunderstanding and unforgiveness can lead to and adopt a bitter feeling in a marriage because the burden that each one carry and bring to the table lead to misconception that cannot reproduce new growth in the relationship but hovering around and over false hope by producing false images and results. Couples lose out on the concept that Christ's healing power awaited them if they give up the wrong for the right and move within the constitution rights of Christ.

Therefore, all the freight and load that we carry equal our burdens, and they will continue to be our uphill challenges. By taking care of your heart, body, and soul, our mind will fall in line, and our lives will be accountable for our actions. If we limit your negative thoughts and put our whole heart into the Lord, we can overcome any obstacle that we might face. The scope of God love is not clear if you cannot see beyond your own faults. As the gross weight of our past and present become your load there is no wonder that so many marriages find they cannot climb over their own mountains or crawl out of valleys. You can see that life's misfortunes can go back and forth around hills because sin got you busy dealing with yesterday turmoil.

As we feel the emotion of our marriage, we concentrate on the axle that it pinnacles on. There are points that cause trouble and problem as it swings back and forth in the marriage. The total weight without substance will not equal or measure up to any contents that will help the marriage to grow. Most marriages at this point will equal stormy weather. Otherwise, everything in the human form that is brought to the table and used will produce a product that is unfruitful in the marriage and leave no ground to stand on and grow, and the marriage will start to draw up and wither away.

If the Lord is not the center of gravity or balance in your life, you might find yourself spinning your wheel in an upside-down world. By letting the Lord be your visual display of unit, you can find peace of mind during your turmoil. Your weight is balance for or against the load you are carried, and your freight will be forgiving. The Lord will show you love that will equal a normal daily walk, whereas your journey will be treated as a blessing.

As God our Lord begin to turn things around in your life and, he will make moves that will represent his true love that goes beyond our understanding. As he begins to remove the very thing that is causing us to struggle and look the other way, He will because your bridge across trouble water. He is the one that can deal a winning hand and within his winning hand are your blessings. As the Lord begins to subtract your totally weight (sins) from the gross sanctifies (cross) of his love. The true value of your net worth comes forth as pure gold. This procedure of God love will also help you to understand and identify the over the top (is where He is still looking out for you) and shortage (is where He is carrying you).

When you are trying to use outside storage facilities (information's) that is contrary to the word of God, disapprove is likely to be the result. As God's approach the center of gravity in your life, He will be the balancing formula that you can depend on and propelled you to move forward in your marriage. Under no uncertain condition can you replace the Lord with worldly understand and call it success in the Lord name. When assertiveness in marriage flares up, marriage will because hazardous, and if they are not defused or allowed to ventilate at some point, the marriage will become explosive.

Because God has a moral purpose for marriage, and when the rules of the marriage are broken, the laws of sowing and reaping applied. You cannot do anything in a marriage without paying a price for stupidly. Ethics and morals are based on biblical knowledge and human wisdom. Your roles as couples are to seek to understand their purpose and play within the boundary of understanding the decisions that they make and how it can affect their livelihood.

"God love will impact your life anything outside of His love is a pretender of love."

Love Abides With You.

Proverbs 16:11 / Job 31:6

"A just weight and balance are the Lord's: all the weights of the bag are his work."

"Let me be weighed in an even balance, that God may know mine integrity."

Spouses need to see a value in their marriage that they can stand on and build on, regardless of what struggles they are facing.

There are things a spouse needs to see and believe in, in-order to develop a promising marriage.

Let your spouse see the Lord in you.

Let your word be your bond, yes and nay.

(Do not speak against your marriage, double-tongues

Be devotion and commitment on all levels)

Your word needs to stay alive and be encouraging to each other by working together for the cause of the marriage development.

Good leadership in marriage promotes effective communication and fellowship through worshiped.

Do not look at what you can do for your marriage; know what you can do for your spouse.

Shared your marriage in a way that had purpose; show love and be helpful in your communication with each other.

Encourage each other through prayer and through difficulties.

(Pray for each other in and out of season)

Baptize the marriage as a messenger of God's love; keep your marriage intact through adoration and praise by being there for each other.

Your purpose is to grow maturity through discipleship by taking marriage to the next level.

Keep the Lord alive in your life, and let him be the key in your marriage and marriage, the corner stone.

Unclassified information in a marriage can be harmful if not used in a suitable manner to strengthen the marriage. Mindfulness in a marriage can bring great rewards by combining praise and worship together. Never see your spouse as the weaker vessel in the marriage, but see them as a cup you can drink from and pour into. This can be a dangerous signal if the marriage is taking for granted or, taking the wrong way or looked at with little or no value. At this point, the marriage can be exploited and misused until it becomes explosion.

"In order for a marriage to grow, couples must make an open investment and be willing to stay the course."

The Lord weighs our heart with honest scale, and he sees your sincere heart. The Lord put balances in place as a safety net to hold you in case you slip or fall. You can watch your life flash before your eyes and yet not see the true meaning of the Lord true and divine love that He had for you. You can be on the right side of the road but walking in the wrong direction. Service to others is a big part of Christ movement in your life that he is trying to get you to understand that is not about you but how you service others that you see every day. The Lord enjoyed the special bond that he created with you and others He has put in your life. Within those balances, God see where you are coming from and where you are trying to go.

The Lord is trying to bring you out of your darkness into the marvelous light by unbinding you from your past. As you start to expound God's love you will begin to see further into your future because you are seeing through your past into your present that add up to your future. The blood of Christ is the scale of measurement that balances the existence between the now and forever. One of the biggest problems with balancing God's love is our ability to let go of the past and move forward with a cheerful outlook. The weight and load that we carry is the burden that is holding us back and down. If we understand the true meaning of God's love, then we can step away from and out of our shell. Our sinful acts are a combination between our ability to do right and our unconscious state of beings to continue to do what is wrong by refusing to give up its state of beings.

Without him, our existence would be worthless and would service no purpose. Selfish lovecombined by unhappiness can never be true ingredients for true self-motivation. God's love is a form of forgiveness that humanityneeds to experience and let go of to grow and develop into spiritual grown that the Lord can use daily. Human form as we know it today would be non-existence if the Lord never had step out of heaven into our little world and redeem us from our sinful nature.

Couples will encounter many deceitful forms of lifestyle that will feed and create a unique way of thinking, if they let sin rule their way of living, they will become a sufferer of their own deed. This form of thoughtlessness will lead to dismantle a marriage while slowing breaking down the morals of God's instruction for the family completeness. The social structure of lives would be unbalanced, less fulfilling, and non-transforming. If God's is not in the plan for re-establishing love reconnect, disrespect will start to exist. Few human emotions had stayed intact as the flood gates of disappointment led couples to challenge the constitution of marriage.

These struggles sometime refuse to fade away while the soul fights through loneliness and deal with the sorrows of the heart. One of the first mistakes that everyone make in their life is trying to live their life disconnected from Christ. There are many underlining pressures that will pull a marriage in the wrong direction and away from being the center of Christ love for couples. An unman heart will ship wrench and cause great damage to the family or any associate they might encounter. Without understanding needs vs. wants, it is easy to become commonplace, settle-for-less and because broken property of broken heart that life is passing by.

We need to learn to take time and care for our marriage. Sometime, that is impossible because we refused to take care of ourselves less-long someone else. It is important to find time for each other and stop giving excuse for not reading the Lord's word for your marriage, in your marriage, to carry our bad habit and behavior into and through our marriage.

Participating in activities, hobbies or pursing interests that stimulate your creative side can bolster your marriage juices. This level of energy can leave you with a feeling of personal accomplishment and satisfaction that you know that the Lord you believe in can come to your rescues and carry you to a higher level of achievement.

Learning to balance God's love is being able to cope with the pressures that life forced upon you. Christ should be your devotion to life, your devotion to praying, and one you can talk to about anything and hear from at anytime. He should be your daily bread that you take and the cup that you drink from routine. You should meditate on his word before and after, and throughout the marriage to strengthen it.

There are moments we talk to ourselves, examine our pain and hurt, then we look back, and the thoughts break our heart repeatedly until we cry again. The problems that we face cannot be undone and fix with normal hands. Sin has let you in on its true purpose, its pain and all your times of hurt and difficulties start to run into one. The Lord is listening to our complaints and how our heartbeat through our daily walk. In couples' weakness, the Lord is willing to strengthen us in our time of doubt and through our struggles, we pray for support and help. The Lord is and can be a plus in your life that will amplify your progress to produce a more successful movement in your marriage. Nothing can shake you loses from the love of God but you. If the Spirit of God lead you, you can stand on a solid rock andface the test of time.

If not, your life, your family, your children, your work, and your involvement without Christ will never experience a solid base. If you are upset with your spouse and loved ones where all your hurt and pain is placed against them, you will never find anything good in your life to live for. A sinner that is struggling must realize they are paying full price to go to hell, and there is no marriage in hell that have survive the fire.

Everywhere you look, hellish attitudes and activities that relate to hell is free for the taking. So, you think sin is free, and hell comes with a bed of roses, you are sadly mistaken hell comes with a price, your soul. Just think for a moment when wrong never turned right. Only the Lord can make wrong right in a marriage and outside the marriage.

The Lord wants your marriage to be a shining example and a living example for others to see. The Lord can take nothing and make something out of it. He can take your worthless marriage, down and out marriage, your yesterday leftover marriage and reconstruct your marriage in a positive way. Some obstacles you face can cause you the most harm, and why would you continued to live in that type of environment when you have a solution.

So, the best way to balance your life without falling for the tricks of the devil is to put the Lord as the center of your world and let him balance your life where you can lean and depend on him. Putting the Lord first in your life allowed you to overcome your struggles. The concepts of living in the past combined by your present equal your future, but you have no future without the Lord presence. God required us to reconcile our differences and come to consensus. Romans 12:18. We need to balance our life by putting Christ first. This way our life will stay centered and balanced. As the Lord becomes the **center of balance in our life's, we can grow and be on one accord with one another in marriage/relationship.**

Mismanaging your life will corrupt your way of living and, hence, your growth in the Lord and kill your blessings. Sometime marriage does it, sometime a marriage does it, and sometime your association with others does it, and sometime belonging to wrong club and hanging out with the wrong group does it. We need to balance our life in such a way that Christ has our back regardless of our downfalls and shortcomings. The Lord is someone you can lean on and feel 24-7. We cannot depend on humankind to come through for us and wash away our sins that why our soul is important to God.

God is someone who can unravel our ungodly life and restore us to glory. The Lord ability to reach into our past and carve out our present is more than seeing us through and into our future. The Lord redeeming power serves as joy that flow like a river of love through and for us. 1 Samuel 7:12 tell us, "Hitherto hath the Lord helped us, "and he will help us to the end. For his love will bring us one step nearer to the blessed home of peace. Let not your love is cast away, but builds confidence and assurance that the Lord will have your back through it all. Therefore, let us keep fresh in our memory all of God's tender mercies for us and have shown us through his word, therefore, your marriage and relationship will always be balance in the Lord."

Breaking Through

Philippians 3:13

Brethren, I count not myself to have apprehended: but this one thing I do, forgetting those things which are behind, and reaching forth unto those things which are before.

It has been shown that if couples fail to break through their problems and seek triumph over their trouble's, misfortune will continue to linger around their marriage or relationship. Individually and collectively, couples will walk on the edge of darkness. If couples are not willing to forget the things that are behind them, they will become overburdened and bogged down over unimportant things in their presence. Unwelcome news usually comes behind and out of a disengage marriage that causes spouses to break down the essential of the marriage into smaller and it smallest pieces, but the weight of each piece cannot carry its own load. Each mood swings in the marriage will cause a shift in the marriage to override any emotional state of being that couple's may be enjoying for the moment. Over stimulating thought and negative output will cause emotions to overheat and bad attitudes to be refueled.

Developing and maintaining a cheerful outlook can help open doors for Christ to use us in ways that we never thought were possible. There comes a time in life that you got to let go and let Christ managed your situation. There are linking actions in people living that links them to sin. Going along with the flow of sin can be a crippling experience that can be painful. This can lead to complete breakdown of your morals as well as mental state of begins. This process can be a blessing to you as well by defining your ability to see the Lord in you. Your breakthrough can break the chains of misfortunate by opening the flood gate to a true blessing in Christ.

The rainbow of life comes in many colors after divorce, and each color can break the chains of blindness and open blinded eyes to see a new birth and faith in Christ. As you visualize your enemies from a different point of view it is easy to see their true color. It is with great understanding that you need to seek divine help. Breaking down these walls can empower you to see sin for what it is, but that is hard to do when you are walking in darkness and blind because of it. Because sin looks like the world you want to live in and be in, we all fall prey to the sin of the world and the product thereof. A fall can be distasteful, and the way, back up can be long and painful. Friends can and will hold you accountable and misuse you as you struggle to overcome your divorce, and in the same sense, they are more than willing to step on your toes over and over until you see the big picture.

These so-called friends do and say things that can be so hurtful and unforgiving, which in returned create an enforceability experience. These experiences can, in most cases, bring out the worst in you and push you over the edge of your ability to recover alone. Through your heartaches and pains, you need someone that will be there for you and help you to understand your special need. Let your daily bread, while you walk in the faith; strengthen you as the Lord pulls you through your struggles. You can use him in the morning, you can use him at noon, and you can use him in the evening, all night long, if necessary. He will be there for you in the wee hours of the morning. When tears in your eyes refused to dry up, He will wipe your weeping eye.

When you are suffering for reasons that seem unknown to you and, your blessing are far-in-between. And the ground that you are standing on is like an earthquake shaking all around you, and nothing is stable you find yourself crying all the time. It is like the ground has opened, and you have fallen in and troubles on every hand are following you everywhere you go. This is how it is when sin of the world is taking control of your life, and divorce is the result. Sometimes, you feel alone and near rock bottom, and sin is knocking in your door like the DEA. When trouble is stirring you in the face, and daily problems seem endless. As each moment slowly passed by you as, you wrestle with sadness that controls every movement of your life after divorce.

If bad experiences are not fixed within timely manner, heartaches will become life threating. I like to think what the Lord had brought me through will strengthen me, and my pain would not last forever. Name and deeds are recorded in the Book of Life. Your sins are forgiving and thrown in the sea of forgiveness as far as the East is from the West. Salvation is having the ability to enjoy the unspeakable joy that represent the value of your soul.

One day, the Lord will come to redeem those values, and the very essentials of your soul will be spoken in a few words, job well done. For your life lived will be in heaven, so why would you let the soul of another send you to hell. There are sinners who have been going through emotional stress that have hindered their growth down through the years, but they have held on to be wonderful blessing. As you hold on to something that is so real, you can stand the test of time. I see life as a good thing, and there is no excuse to be a loser at the end of your journey because you been through a divorce. The Lord see value in you and able to bless you for your hard work. By maintaining your course of action, the Lord is more than willing to bring you through.

There is no sin strong enough to make you lose your soul over it unless you are willing to give up your soul for it. There is an old saying the higher you go the greater the fall. That is true for some and, but not all. I do not know at this moment what category you are falling into, but questions remained do you know yourself? I know if you accepted the Lord as you are living savior, things around and in your life will change for the better. The very thing that is troubling you will leave you alone, you can live again farther beyond your divorce.

A sinner that is full of sin can change in the twinkle of an eye. As you look for outlets in the wrong places, trouble is not hard to find. As you reach the pinnacle point in your life, and you begin to face the very facts that you can be transform into glory, you can give up the wrong in your life that is hanging around you. Sinners refused to face the truth and learn how to let go and move on during their crisis. Some sinners like to hold on the trouble in their life that way, they will always have something to complaint about or cry over.

Not looking back and passing judgment on others can help you build better characters in your marriage without causing destructed harm to self and your spouse. For my Lord, Grace and Mercy have been extended to me and as well as you, so forgive and live a life that is worthy to be praise is his gift for us to enjoy and take full advantage of. The good news is that you can relearn to live life's bad experiences in a blissful way and live a prosperous and fruitful life.
Mercy is a friend, and salvation is a savior that equal love. The circumstance in your life sometime can dictate to you, and you can find yourself in a cloudy situation. The decisions you make can make or break you down, cripple you to a point of no returned. You need someone who will understand and be willing to help you in troublesome times. Your emotional and spiritual world, at some point, will stop falling apart, and you can mend the pieces and live again.

Your link to the outside world needs to be cut loose and uprooted and haul off to the dump. Sin will kill you softly and leave you with an empty feel and a sense of looseness. Sinners need to be blessed, not talks about, and they need to be helped, not overlooked. There is a voice that speaks volumes, and words will heal. Like wounds that refuse to heal, like an uphill climb that want go away. Life is more than difficulties that keep you going around in circles. Life sometime is more than a struggle that will put you behind the curve ball. The Lord is a way out of no way, a wheel in the middle of a wheel, a shelter in a time of storm that will stand with you in your times of crises and downfalls.

There comes a time in your life that you mustsafeguard your heart. There comes a time in your life you got to live and let go to move on with your life. To get the fulfilled promise of God true love, you must be willing to put your life back in order with the Lord's will for you. Day after day, millions of people continually suffer emotionally, physically, and spiritually under stress of yesterday's decisions. The effect of those decisions can, in most cases, because more harm than good. Because sin blinds you from the start, you will struggle with understanding and through substances that you have little or no knowledge of and how you avoid pitfalls of life and how to overcome them in your hands.

Your attitude about divorce will help you overcome any obstacles that you are facing that have because you to continue down a winding road. Because of life's struggles, you, refuse to get up and seek help in your time of need can leave you down and out. Depending on someone else for a handout can increase your dependency on them and leave you disappointed. Life and living teach us that someone will be there for us, but as life moves into its own state of existence, we soon discover that we are alone with our small way of thinking. A slip or a fall here and there can cause a chain reaction to come occur that might push us further in the quicksand of life's pitfall. These doubts in the form of an uphill climb can be confusing and cause you not to see the truth, and you will refuse true evidence.

The comfort zone that you have made in your home can be a place where you feel safe and secure, but at the same time, you can lose your soul behind it. Because you refuse to move, and divorce has cause you to turn bitter, you can lose your way around your own home. You start to lie to yourself you got everything under control, only to discover that you are living a continual lie. The Lord wants you to understand without him, your life and soul is running the same dead-end course. Your heart will feel like crushed ice and wasted time if you do not change your wicked ways. When sin is holding your life, the results will be sinful and without restitution. Time will walk you down and point out your faults and misfortunes.

After divorce has slowly walked your down and your eyes are too weak to produce tears, then you will try to find or put the Lord first in your life. After years and the pleasure of yesteryears have caught up with you and the love of life has left you defenseless, then you will understand the love of Christ will be there for you, why wait that late in the game to come to the Lord for restitution. But the question to you is why you must wait that long to discover the true meaning of God's divine love (agape) love that has been there for you all along.

If an emotionally divorce has cause you to live in sin, where your life is feeling fruitless and start to spin out of control, then you are not alone. If you have heard this a thousand times, there is a thousand more, sin is not your friend. Sin through divorce will cause to look at your partner with a different of set of eyes and makeover. The first steps you take after letting go of sin is the key to your future and how others view your situation. If sin got you charged up and you are feeling emotionally drained, you will show it through your daily journey. It is extremely hard to turn off old habits and form new ones from old circumstances and conditions starring you in the face daily. When you are living with past situations day after day, situations will begin to look the same. Because marriage failed and the company you are keeping now is looking like before, you are viewing your presence in the past where your past is your now, and your now will look like where you are trying to go, for you have already been there before.
(Deja Vu).

"The company we keep will influence our condition."

If you never change your attitude about divorce and how it has affected your life and what you can do about it, your response and result to life's illness will be the same. If you never change anything around, your things will remain the same in and out of season. It is what has been learned from divorce and how we counteract the situation through our experiences that help us to grow and be more productive in our life and how we live thereafter. When sin has reached through the barrels of life and pulled us into its world of default. We search for hope and try our best to remove yesterday; therefore, we get involved deeper into sin, not realizing sin is the cause of our disappointment and life struggles.

We spend a fraction of our life getting even for things someone else has done to us. Not realizing what we do to others will come back to us in one form or another. The Old saying is true, you cannot escape the consequences of one's actions. Sometimes unfairness rules the nest where your happiness is temporary housing. Overbearing dilemmas corrupted our house and caused us to run from the very thing that can be a healing and blessing for us and others.

The forces between two evils are a drawing magnate that caused the average person to lose their way. Habits from the past and faults in the present can keep us pulling to the left or the right when we should be going straight ahead. We struggle into our future by pulling yesterday past in-tow. By refusing to let go we find ourselves wrestling with our destiny by not seeing our future. As human beings we toss ourselves into sinkholes that leave us confused in a way that we see no way off. In most cases, we fool ourselves into believing we have the answer to our tricky situation.

Troubles in life can bring trivial things into focus and, at the same time, push our lives into a nose-drive. Life with little stomachache can box us in and cause us to view life in a negative way. Life cannot be overlooked or taken for granted, there are consequences for your action. These actions sometimes unlock and unblock the very thing you are determined to get away from. The principal function of living can be reference to forgiveness. Normal behavior can be viewed as a marriage that developed out of love and the sharing of the same between two individuals who are willing to share and uncover their true feeling for each other in a way that will stimulate love and bring it to the forefront of the marriage by developing a continuing state of faith. Believing and having someone that will stand by you is one of the most important essences of God's divine love.

Love is love that is beautiful and creates a relationship that will see you through and beyond your present condition regardless of your trials and tribulations. Love is love that will pick you up when you have fallen off the scales of measure that only faith can measure. When you look at the part, and your heart is falling apart, and your inside is eating away at you. Where are standards that help individuals to develop their growth and, minimize their heartaches, and help eliminate difficulties with which they are struggling?

He will never forsake you or leave you, for he knows what you are going through and how you got there. He will always be there for you. The token of his love surrounds you throughout the day, and every day, your faith will grow in him and him in you. Every day, you will enjoy the bounties of his providence and not overlook the present of his blessing but embrace them with open arms. Therefore, he will always be there for you through your divorce.

Chapter 3
Damaged Goods

Roman 3:23
For all have sinned and come short of the glory of God.

"Giving your all and everything to your spouse, and they give their goods to someone else, and they wonder why you want to tear their head off."

One of the most profound and corrupt operations in the world today is living under the influence of a mate who has a hidden agenda. This individual sole purpose in life is to tamp with your life and make sure you feel worthless and hopeless because they are damaged goods. This individual, if left uncontained, will create a behavior pattern that will feed or create a nightmare in your life. This is a sad, sad case that most marriages refuse to address or discussion. This person blends into your world and occupies time and space to a point with no return on your investment in the marriage or relationship is worthless and useless. Your space becomes their space; therefore, you have no space of your own. Your rights are giving up as a door stopper, a walking mat that only leads into abyss.

Sin is born with the idea that it can get away with anything and not be responsible for trouble that had led to your divorce, and it surrounds chaos. Sin has this idea sinful is better, which equation to a sinful nature that will not bot out trouble in your life. Sin lives at the crossroad and incorporates the essence of your life, which is imbedded in the cross between the living and the dead. It is remorseful to think that you can live your whole life and never experience happiness because you are refusing to get it right or do it right.

I am reminded of an old broken-down house across the street where I once lived and an old broken-down man that once lived in the corner of them on lies and deceitfulness that they built with their bare hands. I found out later in life stories that my spouse told me and the lies that rolled off his lips had no truth to him at all. He took his last stand to defend his honor but his reputation for sin had overpowered him. It is not easy to overcome the grasp of sex and drug in a sinful nature if it had a hold on you, the old man said, I became damaged goods. In a good, meaningful marriage, there are cases where the pit of hell is hard to crawl out of.

I am reminded of a story a spouse once told that he loves so deeply that he would give up his life for. The spoke of her in a remorseful way that would bring tears to your eyes, and the sadness on his face would break your heart to just hear and see the reaction on his face. Her predator's sizzling tongue and the thirst of blood had caused many good souls to fall by the wayside. Her taste for the flesh has influenced humankind alike to come back and bow down to the rules of the flesh. Her reaction to love has caused many souls to spin out of control and end up a prisoner of love. Many sexual predators crave for love and to be love.

Many others look for love in the wrong places and live under pressure to corrupt the very hand that feed them. A predator's life is tangle in a web of street living and distrust. Her life is like frosty leaves in the fall, a sizzling summer day in the sizzling heat and, the coldest night in the winter and a chill in the middle of the spring.

Lost forever in time, and a constant voice told her that her behavior is normal. She lives like falling leaves that littered the very ground that she walks on. You can find extra body parts throughout the park of her life where she walks constantly, webbing every soul she touched. You might be wondering why the park never cried out, and every soul visit the park just watched as she took control. She is like a thousand tongues that speak with the sizzling voice of honey that claim the breath that you breathe.

She dazzles you with her soft voice. Her touch will leave you speechless and feeling hopeless. She shared no blame for your shortcoming or your quick fall into abyss. She is like the desert that is thirsty for the living soul. By night and by day, she hunted for the living. She plays for keeps, and you are her prize. She walks in grace and beauty that no man can resistant. Her hugs and kisses are given freely, for a taste of your lip that ragging the depth of your soul. She gives you what you want, when you want it, how much you want of it until your body cannot take it anymore. She will never let your sexual desires down. She will help you live out the flight surround your imagination.

She could sift your love like wheat. She is sweeter than honey dipping off a honeycomb. Every hour on the hour, she markets her territory for a fresh start and the quench for your desire. She has eyes for you and only you. As life and its co-habitation begin to unfold, you become the victim of her prey. The warning is clear and noticeable, but your ability to move is oblique. In your worst hours, it is your turn to die.

Her smile walks on ice, and the water behind her frozen in time and turn the ground into mud, her touch gives claim to the waves in your stormy life. Your heart skips a beat as your life slowly slips away from you. After that very moment, her touch becomes a web of lies and a mixed desire that will swiftly take your breath away. Her touch hung by a gray membrane that is fastening between your flushing minds.

Her strings have no boundaries that restraint them from the heart. Her purpose is clear to the learner but destruction for the living soul. Love teaches us how to recognize affairs of the heart but give little instructions on how to mend a broken heart. But, of course, we took every word that was uttered out of the mouth of loved ones to be true until we discovered the real reason, they loved us from the beginning. He explains the predator as a sick, dark spirit that ambushes the very soul of man.

What she thought and did no man can explain. The odd thing to me was that so many people visit her daily and lay in the park seeking positive energy. Their belief was that all troubles would be erased and simple go away. The predator was unisex, and her habit of eating her lover invites a strange awe about her. Her touch became an emblem of love that grasps the night. Her love is a reason that is never out of time with the season. She counted on this and lives by her own set of rules. Over the years, my grandfather kept his eyes on the park and warned anyone that would listen to him. Grandfather ran his stick through the drifty silver linen around the park boundary.

As it tore, it sounds like cracking pieces of paper. The park slowly looked and rose on its back legs to fight off my grandfather's approach. The park saw everyone as an intruder and seized the opportunity to destroy anything and anyone that stood in the way of her existence. Many people presume that every human has it is elegantly engineered for ecological survival, whichis far from the truth. Grandfather thought every human characteristic and their behavior played an important part in explaining the assumption of the human truth.

With evolution in mind, it sometimes produces flowers of natural evil traits that would add functional or vestigial desires to one's life. The predator wanted her world to be an ordered room of love, but in the corner of each room, a display of untidy body of web. This irreducible mystery that created a motiveless evil in nature help creates a web of disbelief. Her non-humans' emotions prolong the tiresome idea that life has no value, but at the same time, produce to product that was worth investigating.

The incredibly young and the incredibly old were especially vulnerable to her. Some people seem to die not from the venom but from the infection that may follow her bite. Her last victim struggles and struggles to maintain his maturity and dignity before becoming a victim. In her web of destruction, each victim suffered from a false sense of loyalty. Her eyes send a message that life is just that free to give and take.

She is willing to go the extra mile to win your heart, mind, soul. Your bucking knees will cling to every word that drips off her lip. The wing of her arms will sweep deep down into your very soul and suck the very life out of you. Through the gummy silk of her lip, you will become her prey. Her aggressive move turned a beautiful park into an ugly mess. With the midnight hours slowly approaching and, the morning was yet to come.

I could feel the swelling of her hand around the park as the spirit of grandfather lingered with me. My memories of childhood play a key role in my understanding of the park. My grandfather, who made me feel good about spending time in the park, has taught me well. He never opened or said anything ugly about her. This was the last thing I remember about him, for he, too, disappeared.

Grandfather spoke softly about the woman he knew at the park. His voice moves me the most and still to this day have a profound effect on me. Her emotions and unwanted presence still enlightened me. This, I found out later, was a cure and a blessing dressed as beauty. I was especially encouraged by this for the rest of my life not to take wrong for right. My grandfather lost his brother, and now his life as well in the park. Sometimes I cry, and then there are other times I wonder. Sometimes, I refused to look back and wonder what could have been.

Stop lying to yourself.

1 John 1:8

If we say that we have no sin, we deceive ourselves, and the truth is not in us.

One of the simple mistakes most couples make in life is thinking they can kick a bad habit just by thinking about them. The devil has a way of sitting still and making you think you are on top of the hill. As individuals we depend on each other flaws to overcome our simple steps in life merry-go-round.

We can look at other lifestyles and decide and talk about other people's problems that they are facing and laugh because we are not in that situation. Lying to ourselves, we are better than that and better than they are. You can wait all your life for a person to stop lying to you and spend the rest of your life living inside a box, feeling you have no way out. Lies seemed to follow a human pattern, and the teller of the story, in most cases, is the author of the manuscript.

A liar telling lies had the potential to follow an ordinary pattern of disbelieve because it sounded too good to be true, in most cases, you start to believe the lie because you have heard it so many times. A liar will lie just to lie because they know you are acquainted or at ease with their work. A liar will look down on you and point the finger at you as you need to agree with them. It can be small in nature, or big in nature, but the worse part about it is you are affected by their words. A liar will lie about anything in any form or fashion. Some liars can look you square in the face and be lying from their heart and, looking you right into your eyes and lying to you the whole time. You can give them the benefit of the doubt, and somehow, they screw that up. You can know the truth about a situation, and they will stand there and lie to your face as if you have no knowledge or idea what is being said.

Revelation 21:8 (KJV)

But the fearful, and unbelieving, and the abominable, and murderers, and whoremongers, and sorcerers, and idolaters, and all liars, shall have their part in the lake which burnet with fire and brimstone: which is the second death.

The following are things a liar can said:

First, they lie to themselves to convince themselves.

They can look you in the face and lie to you without blinking.

They will lie to you to get your attention.

They can hold your hand and lie to your face.

They can lie standing up and sideways.

They can lie from sunup to sundown.

They would lie if you were not there?

Under press, people will lie without a doubt.

A relationship without fellowship will never equal commitment from either party involved. If the ground you are standing on is quicksand, you will soon find out what the result of your ability to stand in troublesome times will be like. The moment you start to move without the Lord the, quickly you will start to sink and fall away from your belief. Sleeping beneath your sin is a burden you will keep body lifting or bend, pressing unjustifiable. Weight on your shoulder that is heavy to carry alone can leave you wounded and deep in pain. Loving one in a relationship without fellowship can be suicide or trenchless, that will drive away perfect love from loving you. (2 Tim 1:7 (KJV)) tell us:

For God hath not given us the spirit of fear; but of power, and of love, and of a sound mind.

If perfect love is to communication, it would talk about driving fear from you. By having a shoulder to lean on and a shoulder, you can depend on good love can live. How you love yourself and see others will open doors to a successful marriage or relationship by developing a marriage through a constant relationship with the Lord.

False Liars

Luke 6:32-34

32 For if ye love them which love you, what thank have ye? For sinners also love those that love them. 33 And if ye do good to them which do good to you, what thank have ye? For sinners also do even the same. 34 And if ye lend to them of whom ye hope to receive, what thank have ye? For sinners also lend to sinners to receive as much again.

"Don't choose someone while you are weak, because when you get stronger, you will ask Lord what this is I have got myself into."

False loves are stolen moments, like cheap imitation some people cannot take it or wear it out in public it is like a choker around their neck. This leaves false love to pull the wool over your eyes because your heart simply been stolen. We possessed the power to fool one another. We disqualified ourselves from true love by taking each other for granted. We get mad with our spouse about trivial things that will never mount to a hill-of-bean, and we judge them based on that information alone.

We do whatever is necessary to get our point across with the understanding that false love is pretending that the heart feel something it do not. We dishonor God's love for us by stating that we are acting in a spiritual way but showing false love. We give God a small ratio or percentage of our love, and return, we look for one hundred percentage of his love. The Lord opens the windows of heaven and pour out a blessing upon us, and we received it with open arms but never give back to our spouse.

There is a story that was told by a close friend of mine. He stated that I woke up this morning without you. Tell me, Lord,, what is this all about I been in love from the beginning, so why do I feel like I am being punished. My heart was not feeling love, and it was hard expressing something I could not feel or touch. I was feeling unwanted, I had no meaning, and that I was feeling was ruthless. I was conceited to think a bleeding heart would not bleed out, but how wrong was I to think it would skip me.

How did we wake up this morning acting like stranger, I asked her. We were friends who fell in love back when we needed to love someone, so we held on to each other... Now I am wondering how is that I am feeling so alone when both of us are at home. You act like you do not know me, and I feel the same about us, and we are growing apart, fighting over foolish things. Can you explain how we became stranger after the kids?

After all that we had shared, it feels like we just do not care about each other after all these years. You do not know me, and I do not know you where did we went wrong? What happened to the loving that you promise each other? What happened to a lifetime of commitment or until dead do us apart. What happened yesterday that causes us to stand here in tears?

Where has love goes that it would leave us high and dry with these empty feelings of not belonging to each other? When you search the heart and discovery that true love never live here and all the things you felt was just our imagination running wild with us. We were young, inexperience in love, and our love stop when someone else broke in.

Behind closed doors, we hold tears in our hands, trying to hold on to yesterday's memories. In a state of unforgiving, we struggled just to hold on to the little sanity that we have and while we search our heart for clarity. How do two people say they love each other, then turn around and get a divorce? How can they be so eager to put their business in the street, on face book, twitting and all of that, then wake up and file for divorce to act like they never knew each other?

When you wake up in the morning feeling the pain of yesterday, you cannot help but wonder what this is all about and why it had to end the way it did. It was not long ago you were feeling real love that you thought was so, so real. Now you are screaming and kicking nothing about it was real.

I must face the fact I fell in love with a false lover. I was feeling the strain of missing real love. I was depressed and overwhelm, taking pills just to go to bed. The absence of love was killing me, and I refused to be touched or spend time with my hurt and pain. I could see hurt and pain coming a mile away, and the door unlock, hurting me the more. I was used to love being there for me, so I thought.

I was facing another uphill climb and the possibility of not seeing a way out. It was so hard to believe that our love was not making the cut, and I was feeling like I was addicted to every lie that was told. I fell in love over and over, but false love slowly starts to spin out of control. What once made me blush and smile turned into a devilish trademark? Love was good, and I enjoyed it to the fullest and look forward to the future that we would spend the rest of our life loving each other.

If I knew then what I know now,, I would not be in this situation, wondering which way love go. False love is more transparent now than ever before. I could not sleep at night, and my days turned into struggles. False love moves my heart to the hurt zone from inside out from the outside until it became rude and bashful. My eyes were heavy with tears, and my heart was beating out of rhythm. And my heart is still feeling the sting of that moment that you decided you did not want me anymore.

When you walked into our house that, we make a home and told me I was not the one you wanted to spend the rest of your life with. Our love began to sting and fade away like the tires of the ocean faded into the sun set. Our love traveled the road of injustice and landed on the planet of dishonesty. My love for you was at your beckon call, and I followed your instructions to the tree. You talked about others loving one another, but the hurting part of it we did not love each other.

If I were to call a spade a spade then, that what it was a spade? The late nights at work, and your phone that constantly rings left me with these empty feelings that I should have investigated. There were many things attached to an individual that led into doubt, but I believed in you whole hearted with my soul and mind. I noticed right away there were strange things I failed to follow up that came back to haunt me.

This might include the blank space on their ring finger that is supposed to hold their wedding band. The extra miles that they could not explain or took the time to even try. You try to be understanding and wonder what you did wrong or doing wrong. You would think they would tell you or feel the absent of your presence in the bedroom.

You keep telling yourself love will keep you together and strong, but all your efforts were in vain, and now, where love once existed, only pain resides. There are so many things that are possible and positives about you that I feel lost without you. The Lord knows my heart, and deep down inside, you know I love you and cannot live without you in my life. I was willing to make that sacrifice. Is this why you played me like a fool, because you knew my heart was into you.

One of the things I admired about our love was your ability to look and see the future. But as it turns out,, you was seeing a future without me. As I look back at this, I wish I were there to hold you and tell you how much I really care for you. But I know now that is not possible because we are going in separate direction. I wish I could have known this from the beginning. We could have counted the stars and created our own world around God's creation.

I find you to be an incredibly special individual and hope that things between us never change, but I was not living the kind of life that is worth your love. Hearing your voice is the one thing that keeps me going. I know things are different now that I am there, and you are here but my love for you is the same here, but I am holding on to the wrong thing that is false love. The caring and touching is still a desire and a want that will never die. I need you in my life more than life itself. There is no other that can replace you or make me feel the way you do.

You are the love of my life and a true value that come once in a lifetime. Life itself could not ask for more than what I have now. You are my life support, and my life would be incomplete without you. I wish not to lose that, for you are on my mind. This is my life, and I am going to live it to the fullest, and I desired to live it with you. You have so much to offer, and I hope to spin the rest of my life loving and caring for you. I find you to be extremely exciting and full of new joy. It is hard to express myself when my heart is full of emotions, and with all your kisses and hugging, I do not want my life to end up missing that, but it did.

As the days go by and my love grew stronger for you, I can feel the hunger growing for the touch of your love. I hope life finds you in the best of health and I am looking forward to the end of the day when I come home to you. I thank you for your encouragement and continual growth. I deeply miss you in many ways. What you started, you got too finished and keeps it going until the day we are no more.

I know hours will come, and we will feel alone.

But it will be you that I will be thinking of

In the wee hours of the morning

You will be on my mind.

It will stay that way until the end of time.

I will be dreaming of loving you until then.

Holding you, desiring you, squeezing you

My love will follow a path of the heart.

Knowing that,

It will be you that my heart desire.

There is nothing I would not do for you.

My heart love to embrace you.

And fill the night cuddling with you.

We will spread love as we feel it.

For our hearts will have each other

To hold and cherish

For we will see no end in sight

For time will be ours

    I pounded the ground, looking for a true love. Under debris and waterfalls, I searched the world over, only to find missing parts and a broken heart. Until I found you, I was a lonely man living at the edge of night. While standing in the sun soaking wet with my life flashing before me. I could not feel a thing or relationship to anyone without thinking of you. But this was all a dream, and I was waking up to a nightmare in constant pain. Something was missing, and I know now that it was (you).

I thank you Lord, for what you did for me. For taking me in and bringing out the best in me and by helping me stay the course. You gave me a reason to love again, and my feeling grew day by day. In times of hopelessness and despair, you were there for me and abiding with me. I miss your blessing when I was in a world sin chasing waterfalls and hanging onto yesterday hurt and pain.

There is something else I miss, too; I want to say it on this page. I want to keep it fresh as the day I left you, will you forgive me I was so, so wrong for that. The way you work thing for your help me to feel complete and whole again. I miss you, greeting you in the morning with a hug and a kiss in your unique way when you do what you do. I throw that out the window and walk away from it all. I have those thoughts with me that linger throughout the night into the wee hours of the morning. I want to share my whole life with you.

I say to you, let not waste precious moments on foolishness. Just you and me, we can do this thing call love. Just as the morning come, I do not want our love to miss a stroke. I do notwill you to hold nothing back; let us do the things that we like to do and do well at it. (That is how sure I am of you). I count the hours down until I am back under your blessed. I cannot wait until those moments unfold. There are so many things I miss about you.

If I had to count to ten thousand, I would be breathless. There are so many things that I am thankful for, but one of the most important ones is you. I think of the things we can do together that would bring the temperature to a new high. . At this very moment,, let me put it like this: I feel your lip, your chocolate thighs as, your tongue rushing through my mind. Yes, that is what I want from you and want to do that to you. After counting all the days in our life, we shared together as Mr. and Mrs., Last night was so good for me that I felt your presence throughout the day.

Your body was with me very awaking moment of the day. My eyelid constantly reminded me of the present of your beauty. I cannot wait until I hold you in my arms again. Tonight, we are going to start all over loving each other from head to toe, like never before. I want to feel a part of you that a part of me is feeling now. The hours seemed so far apart since the last time I touch your body, but my memories had not escaped me. I feel you in an incredibly peculiar way the warmness of your body and the touch of lips. Like missing air, my life revolves around you and only you, to a point that I am engulf in the abyss of your love. I can see me in you. I miss your touch and the touch of your lip against mine. I can feel your juicy tugging at me, O how I wish last night was today and your body present with me. I am reaching for you this very moment, where are you, touch me, come closer to me, let me feel you, yes, that the way I like it.

The best in you bring out the best in me.

We are makes for each other in many ways.

It is your body that I need and desire to touch.

Your mind I desire to work with

I want to take my time.

And is it nice and slow?

If it takes all night to get it right

You are the one.

I want to do it with

The day is young.

The night had not come.

Let us start today.

Loving each other

In the shower, on the floor

In the bedroom, on the ceiling

From the back, take it all off.

I do not want to see you with nothing on

I love your body it is so hot.

I want to feel you all over me.

Not missing a spot

Can I kiss you there?

You taste so good here.

You know where.

Let us do it again.

Until I feel you

Let us do it over here.

Let us do it over there.

Let us do it until the morning dew blessed us.

Let us do it again, for our body is not dead.

As time keep slipping into the abyss. My life is struck between imagination and what is real. There are things of which I am not fun. I am a lucky man, better than that, I am a thankful man that I have you in my life. As I see it-, I am more than a blessed individual because I have you to love and be loved. You are important to me in so many special ways that the human mind cannot begin to count or comprehend.

I count the days that I am back in your arm and thinking of the moment when we will be together as one. I see your face every day not only in my dreams but also in my daily walk. You see, I have you on my mind all the time and wish that I were with you every awaking moment of the day... There is not an hour that goes by that I do not think of you in a unique way.

I see the stars at night, and my mind fasten to your smile, and my thoughts are vacant without you. I have this picture of you that have brought boundless joy into my life. As the hour sometime slowly goes away, I find myself constantly thinking of you. I need you in my life. If the moon is in heaven and the sun is shining, I will have moments to love and cherish the rest of my life. You gave my life a new meaning and a reason to live again by doing so, you have brought a new focus into my life, and I am so thankful. You see, my Darling, it is you that make my life worth living for, and it is you that gave my life new meaning. Without you, I am nothing and have nothing to live for. You are my beginning and ending, and there is no me without you.

As I look into the eyes of your love, I can feel the love flowing between you and me. There is no end in sight. This I can live with and grow, facing old age with grace, knowing that you are the one for me. Knowing how about you and my feeling are rushing through the heart and fueling my love for you. That each day unlock a new part of me that my feelings and emotions are feeling the same way, and want you to be the one to fulfill my dreams.

So, I say to you let me be the one that comes and fulfills your dreams that will come true, and you will not be surprised about the outcome of life. From that day on, we can live in happiness because our love will grow wider and deeper. I know you are good spouse because I have tasted your love, and what you have to offer is what I want forever and ever... As sure as the hand of love covers me. I want to be your forever plus a lifetime in time. That way, we will never last time for we will have our time if you want it that way. Do you feel that way or is it just my feeling going through the change? I truly hope not, I would hate to think I am in this along, and my feelings are confused because you are giving me the wrong signal.

Your love is like the growing flower.

In the springtime, when love feels the air.

The warmth of the ground and push upward.

As the summertime breakthrough

I feel the blossom of your love.

Holding me closer and comforting me

A never-ending love that

Find its way through another season.

Where love is in abundance

Where love is endless

To cherish me across the

Chilly nights under the open sky

Where the ground beneath me

Is never covered with ice.

For your love, warmest me

As the wintry nights unfold.

For you are my spring

To establish my love again

To create a never-ending desire

That launched from my heart to live again.

To fill an empty space

Like branches reaching for the arisen

Just your love and mine

Pushing and grasping for a dying soul

A seed of love that is never ending.

A growing love with a new beginning

To touch the sky and love again

For you gave me a reason to love again

I see in you a seed of possibilities and a never-ending love that live-forever through time. And every day, there is sometime new about you that keep me loving you, and every passing minute, there is so much joy wrapped up in it. I see in you the rush of love that passed all understanding, a love that loves forever. I see a beautiful spouse that has the heart of gold that no man should hold but me and only me because I believe in you and only you from heaven, I gave you my love and everything will be all right.

For you are my child. I love despite your divorce I still love you today, tomorrow even into the wind. You are the one that I love to be love and I want that for the rest of my life and for you to be the one. That at the end of the day I will be the one you are coming home to, to end the day and start anew. I want to be the one to give you that love. My heart desires you and only you. I need you in my life forever. For there is no me without you, for you are the one I am living for.

Reaching out and finding out

There are times in life that our beliefs overboard into false limitation, and we move into territory of lying and hurting our loved ones through filthy languages. When you have reached out, and now you are finding out what you thought was true, there is nothing to it, and you are not alone. There are others like you and have been through what you been through, been lied to, beaten down and abused over trivial things that amounted to anything.

We come up short on our journey of recovery because we turn and start to blame others for our shortfalls. Because we believe we are damaged goods, we become poetry in motion. We act out our life on stage and become great performers or pretender. We never exit the stage just become part of today's problem that caused us to stumble and fall. Our love and hatred for one another become turmoil for the living soul and bring hardship to couple who are all right, struggling to hold on to the little they have.

Sometimes, we cannot be the boss best friend or boss based on our past history. We never learn that our experience does not have to dictate to us or move constant throughout our life. Because of our selfish way, we become ineffective in our decision because we are basing our knowledge on false accusation. That is the problem with most couples they believe once their spouse has cheated or betrayed them, there is no recovery. This myth is far from the truth and should be explored.

The allegations that have been brought before them are the truth and nothing but the truth, and no room for gray area in their life. This will set well with them if they have never experienced true love and had love bestow upon them to enjoy and feel the touch of someone that absolutely love them with all their heart, soul, and mind. There is a sadness that is going around, and the biggest mistake that feed the mind that a broken heart cannot mend or heal from tragedy.

I was once told you never miss your well until the water run dry. That statement is one of the most profound and thought-provoking ideas that I can love you and hate you all at the same time. The Lord can lift you and sit you beyond where you are now and put your feet back on solid ground. It is so sad to wake up every morning with sad tears creeping through your eyelids, knowing that the problem that you are facing happens at no fault of your own.

Your plea, beg and fall on your knees, and still it seemed like your prayers go unanswered. The person that you chose to live with for the rest of your life is dealing with issues that occurred long before your time. But now their time is your time, and you are living with the penalties of their actions and activities.

Do not get me wrong, I do understand there are things that happen in individual lives that was not their fault, I am not blaming them, but they could have said something before you said I-Do to them. They could have expressed a concern about your well-beings, but they chose not to. Now, you are living with the consequences of their action, and you are not pleased with the result that life is dealing you.

Then you found out the hard way they were damaged goods in shepherd clothes, and you became the satisfice lamb. But the good news about this is The Lord is your Satisfaction and your Lamb, for He knows how it feel to carry the load of someone else burdens and be willing to die for their cause. The Lord feels you and your hurt.

He is carrying your load.

"Some spouses are so worrisome that a frog will consider committing suicide; then to listen to a spouse croaking sound all night long."

"Understanding a damaged spouse is like seeking knowledge from the bottom of a bottle."

"Once the heart is totally empty, you will get totally annoys."

WHY BROKEN HEARTS BLEED

2 Cor. 5:17

("Psalm 147:3 He healeth the broken in heart, and bindeth up their wounds")

"If any man be in Christ, he is a new creature: old things are passed away; behold all things are become new." One thing I love about the Lord is what he did for me.

When I found out, all the love I gave mounted to nothing, and the one that was receiving it took it for granted that it would always be there for them to play with. When I was going through my doubts and all the time, he was there for me, speaking and walking with me, his love was strong, and I could feel it when he would talk to me about my concerns. He cared for me, and he gives back to me the same love that I was giving. Every day, I grew stronger and overcame my sadness with joy. He saw something in me that I did not see in myself. And he showered me with love, and what I needed it was provided. I woke up one morning, and all that was gone with my heart, my love and my soul was left with hurt and a double load of pain on the floor like a doormat trouble walked all over me, and my heart was on lock down I could not feel a thing. The rest of me was screaming to get out; I could barer open my eyes.

When broken hearts bleed, when broken hearts cry, it feels like you are coming to the end of time. You cannot fall off, you cannot continue to hold on, you cannot let go. You are screaming, but no one is hearing you, when broken hearts bleed, sometimes you stop believing and breathing.

Then, moments later; The Lord walked with me and took me through my difficulties in my failing marriage. He helped me to understand that he would never leave me or forsake me. So, I cannot tell you why my spouse did not see what he saw in me? It is not that I do not trust her; she just did not see a future with or in me. She asked me why I would waste your time and mine on a loser. When I know all the time you are not for me, you will never be the one I want or make my dreams come true. No matter how big your heart is I am just wasting away holding on to empty dreams. She said, I cannot get mad with you, she when on to say, you will never add up to my expectations. You cannot live or be someone else, dreams or be their savior when they see no value in you.

They can make all the promises in the world they are just empty words swinging in the air. Living and dying is in the tongue, and the words that flow from their lips can be. I gave my all only to have it stamped disapproved and returned to sender. You can find a reason to be mad and lock yourself out of your blessing through stupidity... I wanted nothing around me that I cannot feel, including love. She showed me love does not live there anymore, and I cannot wait any longer waiting to receive it. A marriage that never changes will never develop a true strong marriage or eat from the fruit of its labor.

I loved her as a spouse despite her madness, and my love for her stood the test of time. A good marriage builds up treasure in the heart of their spouse for rainy days, while a brokenness marriage will throw it away behind earthly follies and foolishness. Brokenness will never mend if the love of your life is seeking desires elsewhere beside home. When forgiveness is asked for and never giving, the road for destruction has been set. Pipelines that lead to open communications are now a highway that is a closed road to nowhere.

Forgiveness and love walk together love is bigger than a thought. Because love was not meant to be alone for love forgives and allows you to show it and live again. You need someone in your life that will treat you with respect that your heart, mind, and soul deserve. An individual who never changes in a marriage will always be struck in time and never be able to bring forth a harvest that the Lord have provided for the marriage to enjoy.

Therefore, the marriage will never be able to afford the fruit of heaven. An unhealthy portion of sin wills only product heartaches and headaches that will cause the marriage to be in constant needs of recovery. Most people in a marriage never recognize the true values of their spouse or the marriage itself.

This type of marriage is hurtful, and sometime, the only person that might survive it is the one that is running from it. In most cases when it is too late or too far down the road to change or a decision must be made to stop fighting an uphill battle. This can be destructive in a new marriage that just found out they are not feeling each other anymore. The biggest problem with most marriages is that couples refuse to get pass post events, that is the cause of the problem, they chose to live with the circumstances and blame each other for their downfall.

Facing your demons is one of the major steps in overcoming difficulties in a struggling marriage. Different points of view decrease the flow of love in a marriage by pushing it in erroneous directions. But most people are glued to yesterday's point of views and refused to change for any reason.

Old saying is true that tradition is best left alone, but I say to you a marriage that is not willing to change is one that will date back to yesterday heartaches and pain. If you stay close to your spouse, understanding will increase and the marriage will gain from it. Staying close to your spouse meaning you will be there for them no matter what is going on in the marriage or what foes are against you.

Love is always vulnerable BECASUE you are willing to give so much of yourself or willing to change for the one you love. Love should be a gift that give unconditionally and be willing to share with that special someone who is willing to give back in that same manner. In marriage, the bible stated that a man and spouse should leave their mother and father and cleave to each other. Love should flow in one direction as love is expressed from issues of the heart and agree to disagree with each other with love.

If your love is clockwise and the movement of your spouse love is counter-

clockwise, the direction of your love will never be parallel to each other. Love will never meet, and because of that, love will fail and create a lost. Love is not a feeling that is spelled out in four letters, but words put into action to bring out the best in the ones you love with all your heart. Love is to feel free to love without obligation to love with a price, to give and not receive.

When loves to speak of unconditional love and you are abuser of that love, sticks and stone will come your way? Reaching out, trying to stay close, reaching in, trying to stay connected, reaching across, over, and under without closing your hands is hard to do. The Lord wants your marriage to prosper and grow in a different space and time to receive the blessings that is due to you and your spouse.

I am reaching through my heart and searching the world for assurance. You should know by now I been here before. I been through and under and have the faith to know what I know the Lord will do right by me. God's love for you will reflect life, and through life, you will need him more than ever. There are so many factors that work against a marriage.

God's love is love, and to a believer, that is easy to forgive in the name of the Lord. Misunderstandings in a marriage by miscommunicating can be a slow-moving machine that will lead couples down a death end road. You found out the hard way some marriage has no meaning and you have watched good ones and bad ones go down for the count. Getting in trouble behind stupidity is more upsetting the second time around, this proves you have not learned your lesson very well.

In a marriage without Christ couples struggle just to maintain their saneness. Misunderstanding under the authority of sin can put a marriage on roll coaster ride. It is not where your marriage been or the cruelty that it suffered you can overcome that. It is the pure fact that you refused to change for the better that is causing the trouble in your marriage.

It is not how you view your present marriage and how your previous marriage ended will keep reminding you where you been. Faults in a marriage can date back to incident in a previous marriage that may have been unresolved. You feel like your life is running out of time, and the world is against you. While your heart is screaming out and coming apart, you feel there is nothing you can do but cry.

You feel the pressure of yesterday unfolding before your eyes. When your heart is hurting behind foolishness, you have circumstance that are reminders where you been and what you did. I hope you are not judging your spouse by their status, that is unfair to the marriage. Sin's purpose is to push a marriage into total darkness. Satan will do anything to get you to give in to the pressure of the world. When a sinner has sincere desire to do things right, sin has an equal desire to keep you going in the wrong direction. Sin is the biggest chaser in the world of chaos. Sin is always running behind you to chase you down and bring you to ruins. It is true that most spouses come back to apologize for their wrongdoing.

Some offenders of sin become shameful and overwhelmed by their faults, that they will seek out their divorcee or divorcer to free themselves from their guilt. When this type of behavior occurs, there is a need for you to understand that the Lord is working in your favor. This applies to those who are seeking the Lord to change their life. In their own sinful ways, they are trying to give up the wrong to embrace the right. On the other hand, giving up their evil habits is a constant struggle for them. You do not want sin standing between you and God's plans for your life. Your destiny should not be governor by the nature of sin but in a way that the Lord can use you in a positive way.

John 12:32 stated that if the Lord be lifted from the earth, he will draw all men unto him, and that mean you. Forgiveness is the first and, furthermost, the greatest misunderstood concept in the human concept, which is simple overlooks when it comes down to the movement in Christ. God died for our sins through the eyes of forgiveness this allowed us to ask and be closer to Christ. It is with profound respect that the cross of Calvary stood for the redemption and the salvation of man sin, that we might have the right to live again.

As the mystery of redemption begins to revitalize our minds and, the goodness of God's grace and mercy become the repenting power that we need to be truly transferred out and from the curse of divorce. Some and cases, after a marriage had fail, hobble around point-of-views that had been miscue and take out of context within the scope of the marriage. Believers do things to change for the better, and others do things to change for the worse because of their misunderstanding and false purpose in their life.

"The principles of sins aren't to make sense out of a false marriage but push deceptions and devices of false evidence in the marriage to support its causes."

When false connections lead into unreasonable questions in your marriage, it can cause drama for you to deal with later. Sin fight against love to prove a point, and every time you let sin rule, you are the loser. Because sin played by a separate set of rules that reflect its purpose and goals that will leave you with an empty feeling belonging. Sin is a rule that goes against the heart in a way that the heart lives by a distinct set of rules.

You can stay close in a marriage but at the same time be misunderstood in a way that cannot explain what the heart is feeling. Stop looking for a reason not to change, just change for your own sake. A new person is always giving birth in the moment they decided to let go of their past. The riches of the Lord's love and salvation redeemed you while you were standing in the way of yourself. You can erase your doubt and give way to a new birth in Christ. When the Lord is for you, the world cannot do you any harm. You can move forward and press on with the prize.

Going to bed mad

Eph 4:26-27

26 Be ye angry, and sin not: let not the sun go down upon your wrath:

27 Neither gives place to the devil.

The honeymoon is over, the representative of true love has left the building, and you got what you never signed up for, the true person themselves, no more playing nice or acting like they care. No more long night pillow talk or making love to the wee hours of the morning or playing in each other's hair or smoothing each other's head. You once had what it took to be each other's lover and be there for each other. Now your world is coming apart and living in separate worlds that are drafting out to shore, and the mere mention of their name drive you insane. The endless arguments that, combined with a constant tit for tat attitude, pushed the marriage into overdrive.

When there no commitment to see where you are going, there is no reason to view your future. You cannot help but ask yourself what really attracted me to this person. Now you know how wars get started and sometime need end until someone is hurt or put in a position to hurt someone. Feelings and depression come like a mighty wind tossing and turning your world around and out of focus. You have been here before, and now your soul can find rest despite your upbringing.

The journey becomes painful, and you must now oversee your heart to get rid of yourself doubt that has created a rotten moment in your life that led to misery. You vowed to yourself this would never happen again to you. Love and hate are a foolish game and no matter how many times you play it, you will never win. You will become another victim of the divorce club when love has run its course, and it is all summed up by one word…DIVORCE!

Do not go to bed mad because you will wake up mad as hell with the problem that you lay down with. The butthole that you call spouse will start to kick you in your buttock, and I mean deep in your butt. Your marriage will go into overdrive, and madness is the result. Going to bed with trash on your mind is a crippling thing that can only produce ruined fruit in the marriage. The first misunderstanding in a marriage is overlooking the pitfalls of the marriage.

In most behavioral patterns, the spouse is taken for granted. Neglect is one factor that supports the evidence that there is something wrong with marriage. We see what we want to see, and the rest we overlook or, play down or pay no attention to. What we lack in communication we fuss and fight about inside and outside the bedroom. What we lack in getting to know each other will spill over into our daily living and, in more cases, cripple the marriage.

Downplaying is a method in marriages that can produce a false warmness that can ruin a marriage because no one is taking blame for errors in the marriage. If messages are left unchecked and out of focus, they can mangle a marriage helpless. A cold heart can easily drift off into the sunset under the coverage of the night and leave their present condition fighting for support.

If falsehood can grow roots in a marriage, the true meaning of dislike will have couples refusing to face the facts that there little left to hold on to. This can corrupt the true meaning behind feelings and dull your ability to think how to survive the marriage. A savaging marriage can be just that, and the worst of it all is when two individuals refuse to work on their own marriage but always willing to help others in their time of dilemma. If the marriage is based on love, honesty and trust, then where does loyalty come in.

Our mind will become a pillow of salt that will drive you insane at some point or another if not dealt with within the guidelines that govern that marriage. As the condition of your marriage plunged into despair and spiral downhill, helpless is where couples often give up. Couples normal understanding become unstable, and they see things from a different perceptive. This leaded into a whole new set of rules that only applied to that state of mind you are in.

As the rest of your life fall into upheaval reaction, we often draw the conclusion that life is not worth living. If this problem is not dealt with quickly a good marriage can go bad in a brief period. As the unforeseen begins to come into focus, in one way or other, years later, you will have to deal with it. The day it all come tumbling down around you may be the day that you are down and out. Your eyes may be blocked or closed, and your heart is the only thing that you can feel, but life will not make sense to you at this moment. This will become the sad day of your life, and moving on will be hard to do or manage.

However, to understand the full effect of the marriage one must look inside their heart to understand the adhesive that is bonding the boundary of the marriage together that is falling apart. This is hard to do once the chain of communication is broken and left to ruin on the grounds of blame. Years will pass by, and you will still be wondering what went wrong and where it all went wrong. At this point, life will turn into an uphill climb and force you into reality. You will do everything in your power to hold on and make things work for the sake of your own sanity. This struggle with life is a short-term solution that can lead to depression and sadness. Therefore, you need help with self.

As life pushes you to the edge, you will feel hopeless and without focus. The real pretender of the marriage will rape and rip the very life out of you. You gave thought to your heart with the understanding that love will return, but your soul will continue to hurt the most. The sinner of life with their sins will pretend that they love you and be willing to take care of you. Just as your life is coming through and seeking a breakthrough, sin steps in again and wrestles you to the ground. Let me shout, scream and take my frustrations out on you, sin said with a deep and compelling voice. Then, the pretender just up and walks away, blaming you for the downfall and crises in their life. As you realize the importance of life's pitfalls and, the very thing that you are trying so hard to get away from will never stop chasing you. You look for solutions and apply only the thing that you think will help you only to discover that life has faults of its own (you).

Not because you have discovered a new you but because you have come to realize that life has more than being slapped around and dogged out. You do stand for something; you do have a standard, and that is you. The complexities of life and nature of depression with the onset of fear can leave you feeling helpless and create a deep and everlasting dilemma. There are few things in life that you can hold on to and enjoy the fullness of without sequences and pitfalls. The solution lay with you and the mate you have chosen. When depression sets in, and your emotional state of mind starts to chase waterfalls, you can you blamed if you let this happen.

When thoughts of life become the victim of foul play, nothing can be said that will ease the pain of yesterday. When tears from your eyes fill the room of despair and hopeless screams from the ground, unlocking the past, uncertain mood and swing come into play. You must start to face the reality of life's difficulties by putting life back into perspective. Being careful is the farthest thing from your mind and worse condition you can be in.

Couples have tendency to reach out for help and draw other people into their problem that cannot help them or do anything about the situation they are in or living. Most people who know you will step back from you at this point. They are not what you want or need in your life because they are ordinary people with their own personal issues. Some individuals have nothing to offer or give that will help you in any way that will clear up your thought process. It what you feed your body, and through the eyes and mind, we are connected to the spirit of another lifestyle that, in most cases, will make us sick and unapproachable because of the language that is being spoken.

If you feed your body and mind against the spirit with sinful things, then you will escape the consequences of one's actions, and deep healing will never take place. Only when the spiritual mind is renewed, a change will take place and bring about a change. Your soul is searching for lifeline and a need to lineup with the Lord's plan, with that said, the Lord's plan should be your plan. The impact of your reaction and interaction will uncover the very essence of your existence. If the inter-the evildoers of a lesser God have touched you, then you will find yourself serving a God of darkness.

Nevertheless, to overcome the very thing you are trying to run away from, you must deal with it head-on. Facing the problems and overcoming them is easier said than done. With years of experiences and know how this is one task that is hard to do or erase the pain of yesteryears that led up to this moment. Grandfather always said; to be touched by sin; is to see it for what it is, if possible, move away from it in a hurry.

Things not to carry to bed with you:

Do not carry your ex-marriage, ex-friends, ex-affairs, your ex-attitude to bed with you (stop sleeping with the enemies) your ex's is someone else problem, not yours anymore. (Do not keep your exes alive by letting them back in your bed or giving them strength and domain over your body.) move on

Never sleep on the top of the cover when your spouse is under the cover. This show separation

Tell your spouse up front we need to talk, and please stick to the subject at hand.

Bring up the past only as a reference clause or to put clarity to a picture that you are painting so that your spouse can see and engage with you as you dialogue with them. The past sure proves a point that a spouse should be able to relate to in common sense and the present circumstance.

Talk about today issues in a timely manner that will allow you to go over the issue with respect or set time outside the bedroom to discussion issue(s), it hard sleeping with one eye open.

Consider your spouse feeling and how they must feel walking around with unsolved issues, take notes by using mental or physical notation, or produce a method that will work well for you.

Be open for suggestion outside the bedroom by moving in a positive direction forward and with your spouse in mind.

A COUPLE OF PITFALLS

Jeremiah 48:6

Flee, save your lives, and be like the heath in the wilderness.

"Just because you rate yourself had a ten doesn't mean your spouse is a happy camper."

Self-love is not self-assure, just foolishly thinking:

I heard an old man say in his last relationship, he saw the big picture, but before that, his eyes were closed to any possibility that the Lord was seeing what he was seeing. Therefore, he always thought the Lord was looking the other way when he was hurting and screaming out for help. Consequently, he ruined everything he touched, including his marriage, job, and family, because he never saw the big picture until the very end.

I want to save you this headache by helping you put the right emphases on the focus of life you can see and be a witness to new growth in your marriage. If the focus of life is off base, your way of living can turn into chaos. There are certain rules in life that life follows regardless of self-rules. If you do not put your life in order, things will start to fall apart before your very eyes. And you can bet your bottom-dollar your life will turn upside down and inside out on you. All that you even thought and did that you thought you got away with will start pouring out of you in a horrible way.

The following information can be costly in one form or another if not used in a fashion to fight uphill battles in your marriage.

Active ingredient: "Put into play how you see your spouse and what your spouse sees in you, what you are made from and what you are becoming through loving them and show it. It will be at your best interest that your spouse will see the good in you."

Mission: "Walking together in Christ is by building a marriage that will stand the test of time in praise and worship; that incorporates the heart, soul and mind to stand on a solid foundation."

"Visions: "Visions are positive steps with positive ideas and achievable goals that you agree upon in marriage to achieve full partnership."

"As you live out the mission of marriage and the vision that the Lord given unto you. He will open the windows of heaven and pour upon you the fullness of his love."

Have you ever found yourself disconnected from your Bluetooth or any other device that you might have. Have you ever found yourself talking to yourself aloud, and no one is listening to you, and everyone that saw you thought you were ridiculous. This is how the Lord hears you when you are disconnected from him. Hello, hello, hello. Anyone there, can you hear me, do you hear me, hello, hello, hello. They must have hung up. When sources of communication around your lifestyle are cut off, things will start to look different and act different, causing the marriage to disengage.

Ruining a marriage is acting irresponsible or behaving in a way that will destroy your own way of living or killing any chance of success, credibility, or effectiveness in the marriage. Pitfalls in marriages are designed to compel marriage into a new direction with the understanding that mistakes can produce growth. Couples often find themselves in a holding pattern that will distract the movement within the relationship or create negative results that would be devastating to the success of the marriage. The nature of pitfalls comes in two-fold self-defiance and self-destruction.

When couples become their own downfall, disobedience and rebelliousness will push them into a corner, where the marriage will start to struggle. Some couples' way of thinking is abnormal, and it shows in their way of action because of their childless and mindless thoughts they always end up as destructive behaviors. Couples will start to lose trust in their relationship when they are not willing to work together to bring down the curtains that will open the doors to healing.

They will continue to struggle with the insignificant things in life and their eyes and heart will never be on the same page or never open wide enough to see their faults. Most couples find themselves struggle behind foolishness dilemmas that they refuse to face. This type of humiliation will leave them wrestling with the impossible of overcoming their own fault.

When couples refuse to work together to conquer dislikes and misbehavior within the marriage, stress will start to erode the marriage. As daily functions cause you to feel helpless and hopeless you may not see or feel there is a way out of your dilemma but to fight your way out. Some couples like to argue. Some live to fight with their partner just to leave them wounded and feeling powerless. Some start bullying their partner by humiliating them in public. All this leads back to how individual see each other in their relationship that we call marriage.

Couples have tendencies to talk about each other in negative ways. This method is not conducive in a relationship that is trying to fulfill the marriage obligation. Unhealthy habits should be talked about or be aware of or observed before couples say I-Do. This will help eliminate any ill-manners in the relationship before marriage takes place.

Unhealthy habits can open doors but, at the same time, minimize any resentment or attitude about moving forward with the marriage if talked about beforehand. If a spouse violates the quality of your love, your love will start to disappear, and irritation with the marriage will start to kick in.

Because there are parts of your spouse that has limitations, they may not be willing to push the envelope to the next level. They might not be willing to fight for the marriage but walk away from it or search out ways to destroy it. Anti-Social behaviors around the house can turn into hours and hours of false dialogue.

When a behavior is controlling in a relationship and behavior itself is out of control, one or both spouses will find their goal hard to deal with or keep under press. When the relationship is not streaky clean, most spouses will encounter troublesome times and struggle to stay upbeat in a tough situation.

Couples will find themselves continue swimming upstream against the current of the marriage. Marriages are based on how communication is processed and information is used. Because communication has a language of its own, most couples speak and talk in tongues to each other, then belittle them. These hidden feelings will not allow couples to express their true love through normal channels of expressing.

out your dirty laundry is one pitfall that has caused so many couples to self-destruct. It is one thing to say I do not love you, but it is another to put it into action. This is where the problem lies and where couples start to hurt each other through words and false actions. Cruelty steps in reiterate open your heart to experience downfalls by becoming a victim of its own or resting in the arms of its enemy by circumstance.

When your life became more than abnormal behavior, there are patterns that create levels of misunderstanding that applied more pressure to the marriage downfall. Vindication can take root in a marriage, and a nasty attitude will take on a life of its own. At some point, brutality steps in and hand-to-hand combat creates sudden death in the relationship that can kill the marriage in its footsteps.

Creating boundaries in a relationship before marriage can signify that you refused to participate in foolishness and gossip in the marriage before you say I-Do. Pitfalls are not designed to keep your image and reputation intact but designed to help you to see the overall picture that will keep you from falling for the same old thing repeatedly in the marriage.

Pitfalls do allow you to stand again and be strong in troubling times by holding on to God's unchanging hand. For the Lord see your mistakes and where they have taken you to the pit of desperation. Your mission, if you decided to accept it before you say I-Do, is to keep creating movements in your marriage that will allow the marriage to grow and maintain its vision, mission, and core values to develop a more adhesive marriage.

Individuals in a relationship need to develop an open mindedness to their marriage to be a grower in the marriage that will push the marriage to a level of full potential. By helping each other, spouses you can show one another they can depend on and have confidence in one another. As couples come to know each other they should create a bond that is unbreakable. Matthew 19:5-6 tell us that combining as one in Christ is leaving your mother and father and cleave to one another and becoming of one flesh, rule in the sight of the Lord, we become as one before him. But this occurred in the heart, soul, and mind of an individual before they say I-Do. You must see your partner before they become your spouse, that completes your life.

Doors of communication should never be closed at any given time, but a knob to understanding that will unlock the possibility for the heart and soul to live and grow in Christ. When you believe in one another and promote one another, you have gained one of the most important steps in conquering marriages false behaviors that betrayed you.

A grower is not defined by their job or status in the community, but by their relationship with Christ and their spouse they believe that the Lord had blessed them with. A grower in the house for the Lord builds a home for all to live and be a part of growth. Noah did not build the art alone, but with the measurement of the Lord, he was able to stand and build on the Lord foundation.

This is the same measure the Lord is building into you, just take his word and build on it by applying the living word in your marriage. The Lord wants us to stand and build a foundation that will stand the test of time in our marriage. Therefore, when the storms of life come, we will be able to withstand them.

The Lord has a desire for us to live holy in his name and be a part of his kingdom. The Lord gave us the bible with a blueprint that we can follow and become a part of in a way that deserves of his praise. By building our marriage on the foundation of the Lord standards, we have a great treasure in the blossom of the Lord that is immeasurable.
A grower is not intimidated by the success of their spouse in the Lord but embraces the growth that brings them closer to the Lord.

A grower is not an individual in the marriage that sits on their hands and lets the world dictate to them. A grower does not blame other, nor do they belittle the house that they live in or the spouse the Lord has given them to cherish and love forever, not as a steppingstone or door mat to walk on. They gain favor from their spouses by seeking the wise in the wrong they have done and learn from their mistakes that the Lord can use the worst in us to bring out the best in us.

"An ex-spouse, in some cases, is not willing to give up what they had enjoyed for someone else to enjoy, that is why some spouses keep hanging around. Not because they do not want it back because they do not want you to make good on promises they could not keep.

When you are operating in a stressful situation, there are times that leadership and decision-making are not equally shared. This will compound the discipline line of communication and allow it to be restricted. The marriage will become inflexible and unbendable as the strokes of the marriage take its toll. A radioactive marriage is marriages that generates a faulty product or residue that linger around the marriage for years to come, and sometime couples never get over their exposure. These emotions and heartfelt feelings are left-over after the finishing stages of the marriage have reached its boiling point that keep reminding them of yesterday's activities. Nothing is safe outside the marriage, and nothing is off limit in the arena of the marriage. When two individualsare not on the same page, outside forces can easily corrupt the marriage and create pitfalls that they will struggle to overcome.

Everything at this point will become toxic and wasteful. At this point trouble will come and set up resident in your heart and seek opportunity to take control of your daily walk. If things stay out of focus and continue to be mishandled, the safety net that you thought you had will never materialize or come to be. As safety matters begin to be decoded by subject matters, things will become explosive by any means necessary.

Carrying a torch to rob, steal and kill is the devil's device to cripple a marriage by using homemade tools to destroy the very thing you are working so hard to build. A good report in marriage is based on

Christ. Within each other, there are pressure points or pitfalls we need to avoid or spend a lifetime staying away from to remove the clutches of the devil's tools.

There are three major players in life that keep you balanced. It is like a triangle: church life (spiritual life), family life (your support of love, meaning) work life (peace on and around the job). When one of these levels is off balance, you are subject to be a push over the edge. If you are blending or staying together for support reasons, you can be balanced. But if your life is upside down in any form or other, your life will because a balancing acts in some cases worse than tight roping. If you become unbalanced at any given point, in any direction, you are subject to fall.

Occasionally, everyone gets knocked off their rocking chair and unable to move due to their fall and, the distance the fell from, and what caused the fall to take place. If love is on a one-track highway and only felt in one direction, it would be hurtful and painful to the very end. Love goes in both direction's forgiveness and forgiving. If you never learn to give and receive, you have no way of recovering from a downfall.

If a person learns to give, they can stand up. Forgiving allows couples to reach up and reach out to receive God's empowering power to walk upright in grace and mercy. If a person learns to receive, they can stand to give, this way, they know how it feels to rise. Sometimes, you are left with the sting of yesterday and the bad decisions that have left a bad taste in your mouth. If we, ourselves, cannot reach out to others with the same love, then our life will turn out worthless and endless because there is no room for the Lord to forgive you because you cannot forgive others who wrongful use and mistreat you.

If we become bewailing and confused under the umbrella of commitment to each other, then what is the point of ourselves when we cannot love another with forgiveness. We stand alone. The possibility of our marriage without Christ is so low on the survivor meter that it is invisible.

We all get off balance at some point in life, it is how we put ourselves back on track and back together that will help us to maintain the marriage that will make all the difference in the world. Have you even made up your mind about it sometime and then changed your mind about it? The outcome was the best thing you ever did in your life. Then again, on the other hand, it turned out to be the worse decision you ever made in your life. So, what were the causes that outweighed your decision to move one way or the other? There is nothing wrong with your decision in the way it was processed.

One question you might ask yourself during all the heartaches and pain that you are going thought is. Do you have all the information or understanding to make the right choice, or just half of the facts that led you to your judgment? Without a reasonable doubt, life can throw you a curve and watch you swing out. This curve is called sin, and guess what you will never win at the game.

The information you are relying on is false information that can corrupt your life and, how you live it and how you will finish or run the race to the end. Most individuals, in your case, struggle with the idea of changing their lifestyle or moving to the next level of understanding that sin does not need to rule their life. This is where most problems and trouble start from. Making the right decision can be troublesome and a taxing one.

In moments like these, most mistakes take form and move into the unconscious state of mind where it takes residence and live forevermore. Sin with tell you your secrets are safe there. Only if you know there are no safe secrets in the unconscious state of mind eventually it will come out. One of the great mistakes in life is when we fall and where we fall. I look at life as if no one is there to help you, and you must be willing to help yourself. Butyes, there is butt, this where the Lord comes in at and works it out for you.

You see, we all make mistakes and try to walk away without the hurt and pain. But let me tell you, you are not balanced. For the wages of sin will come full circle in your life. So, you must learn how to balance your going and coming. We review our lives and living until we reach a point where we cannot go any farther. We can jump, run, hide, and climb the higher mountain until we fall. The Lord wants you to succeed in every area of your life, not just in running but standing still, not just in jumping but in walking upright, not just in hiding but being a spokesperson for him. He wants you to be a living example of what he can do with nothing, not just a mountain climber, not just a valley of dry bones, but a bridge across trouble water.

I look at the importance of life, and I see valleys and peaks that I know I saw no way out of or around, but look at me now. I am a witness to what God can do and willing to see you through. As you gather your thoughts, let me add one more thing to this equation and that is the Lord will never forsake or leave you alone to fight your battle in times of despair. He will be your refugee and shelter in time of stormy weather. As I viewed the other side, I am better off than yesterday, and my today in brighter, and I know tomorrow is not a promise to me.

I am living for today in today that if tomorrow does come I will be blessed and better prepared for the future. I am facing the real facts of my life but not at the expense of others. There are decisions I made in my own that, to this day, that still hurt, but I am learning to deal the fact it my fault. The way was not always clear for me, but by God's grace and mercy, I am able to see better days.

You see, I read the handwriting on the wall and plain to see that my life was headed in the wrong direction and about the wrong thing. I did not take it personal when the Lord told me the truth. I was blind to the facts that sin was doing me in, and he opened my eyes to what would be and what was to come, and the outcome was not what I was looking for at the end of my journey.

There is no darkness that I could overcome and let me say this with an open heart and with joy that the Lord loves me the way he does. His life and living have set an example of what living should be like. He set me free, and I cannot live or do life without him. He loves me despite, and the more he gives to me, the more I give back, for I am blessed to have him by my side. As I examine the closeness of Christ in my life and his death on Calvary and, what he did for me has open the door for my redeeming in trialing times.

I can only think about all the times I was wrong, calling it right, and he was blessing me. This is where I know the Lord been good to me for, I can see yesterday and what he did for me and brought me through to bring me here. God's love is committed to you and your soul that you will have the blessing of his son. Whatever you got to do for the Lord, go ahead and get it done, you never know, it might be the best time of your life. So, I say to you, keep living with the Lord in mind that way, I will never be without him. He will always be there for you when your life is standing still.

In my moment of harshness, my weakness overshadowed my ability to overcome the very thing that I was trying to put behind me. I tried to apply the only thing that I knew would work. Guess what, I failed at that, too. I looked at it from a worldly point of view and drew from the little knowledge that I had gained through my years of experiences. My wisdom was not wise enough to go through the very thing I was running from. So, that is why my hills turned into mountains and my valley became difficult to cross. This is understandable in most cases like this. We as human beings depend on the very thing that got us in trouble the first time.

As I look back on my previous acts and activities, I can see the handwriting on the wall. But the question remain is why I did not see and understand the similarity of my marriage with life until I reached the low point in my life. There is a beautiful beginning to life, but sin is always pushing against you and rushing to get to the end. I never let the Lord work in my life I was too busy trying to do things my way. Do I need to explain my downfall that led to this moment? You cannot escape the consequences of one's actions is just the beginning of your hurt and pain.

So, I pushed the envelope to the end and beyond that, I saw no limit in sight. You are made of the right stuff, but you are using it for the wrong reasons. All your cheating and lies, somebody got to pay and that somebody is you. I never looked back and took everything that was given to me for granted. If I keep living, I knew one day it would come back to me, but I thought I had a chance to get it right before that day would come.

Farther up the road, when you are old and blue you will ask the question why it took so long. Why did it take *so* long to get on the right track? Why so many difficulties and disappointments to bring me around and out and into the marvelous light of the Lord. You see, sometimes God do not step into your will he just let you go until you hit the wall. Sometime until, your midnights rolled into your days, and you become refused of insignificant things that you cannot do anything about.

Until you feel uncomfortable in your own little world. Until you are moneyless, homeless, carless, sickness set in, you do not figure you need him before then. Still, through you are denied and unfaithfulness, he still loves you the same. When you are going through your pain and hurt, he is still there for you, but you are down and out so bad that you do not feel his presence. You keep crying out but not reaching up he extended his love, and you rejected it. Now, you need his forgiveness, but your mouth cannot speak, and your mind does not work. Guess what? It is finished.

I have always admired the patience the Lord had with me. I know I have messed up more than a few times on this journey. I see a lifetime of blossoms where the Lord has brought me from and through to this point. I am going to let you in on a little secret I have not always been who I am today or, how you know me or how you see me before you. I stand a justice man in court of sin that been redemption through the blood of Jesus Christ, my Lord and Savior.

I can stand and be a witness to what my Lord can do with nothing. I was outside looking in, no food on the table, jobless, standing in the line of unemployment. I would like to pause at this moment to give the Lord a shout out and praise for who I am and where he has brought me from and through. You see, I used to talk the talk but never walked the walk. I used to sing the songs but never from the heart; have you seen it used to be all about me? Just like the Lord always does. I cannot explain it or justify it by any means, just like he does he always does, and he will always be there for me.

There is so many Christians'standings for worldly things by bending at the waist. Never on their knees to ask the Lord to guide their footsteps? There are church members who are seeking the Lord within the comfort of their own understanding only to keep coming up short and without guidance. I been to the end of the line where friends had one up on me, where loved ones give up on me, what hurt me the most they knew everything about me and refused to let go of the past. They are a constant reminder what are wrong with this world as we know it today.

There are friends I got to let go of, places I got to stay away from, things I cannot do anymore. It is the price you will pay for a little thing in life that sin give freely. Sin will put your soul on layaway and come for it later. Sin will pay a little at a time and expect an enormous collection at the end (your soul). If sin goes unchecked, never put in its place, unaccountable for its action, free at will, causing habit to turn into chaos. Sin can cause corruption in the mist of believers. This is the nature of sin unblocked and set free. Sin is not willing to turn back or let go only want you to stay bewildered.

Doers of God's word put faith into action. Psalm 51:11 stated that repentance bring about a change, repentance turns on the light in dark places, repentance will keep you from backsliding behind closed doors. Coming from where I been, I knowing what I know this is firsthand knowledge of Proverb 14:14, where it stated that.

The nature of sin knows no boundary, no limitation, no self-controlling why because this is the nature of sin not to give in or give up on a single soul into force to do so. If sin take control of your life, your action will be out of control. Your life will develop a chaos, and live next door to corrupts by living by the rules of evilness. Sin is unkind and unwilling to let go if it knows it has a chance to inflate your life and take control.

Unbridled sin is sin at its best, and your life is just a stepping stone into challenging times. Unrestrained, ungoverned, uncontrolled by the very nature of sin can leave you facing uncertainly. It is easy to find yourself locked behind closed door, looking for a way out through the peephole of life. You will find yourself isolated from the one God who can help you get through your difficulties. He can search through the debris of your life and bring out the best in you.

At the edge of your life and so much hate is present, we forget there is so much more, and you have the right to live. Lord, as I step forward into a new diminished, I want to see you face to face and hear you say well done. For me to do that, I must give up the olds and step into your plan. Lord, I am seeking your guidance and wisdom to see me through this. I was once alone and without your touch now that I have found, you blessed me in ways I overlooked and took you for granted. I was falling into the nature habitation of sin and not looking back. You unearthed me and set me free from destruction.

I was headstrong in my unique way, only to be a fault of mine, a hindrance to my growth. I prayed not to turn back the hand of time and look back to go back there is so much in front of me that you can bless me with. I have not forgotten what you did for me and rescued me from and how it was done. If I had ten thousand tongues, that would be enough to give you thank. In you, love found away, love found me.

I have struggled with the flesh like so many like me. I put up a good fight only to lose the battle. My selfish reasons were all about me, and no one else counted. Lord, I want you to see through his eyes and help you to get control of your life. I prayed not to fall by the waste side but to hold on to God's unchanging hand that I will stand the test of time. Lord, granted me the strength to form an alliance with you that my soul will escape the unrest that is forming against my heart.

My Prayer:

O Lord thy God I give my thoughts over to you this day that I might grow stronger in you. I see the handwriting on the wall and my name is not there. I like to stand before you this day and declare my wrongfulness and pray that you enlighten me to see a better day to grow and worship your holy name in praise. I know all that I have done and did before you have not been pleasuring, but you saw something in me that I did not see in myself, and you blessed me despite. So, I take this time, this moment, this second to say I am willing to turn my life around and let you director my life.

O Lord thy God, I pray that I see the big picture that you have plan for me to be and become, in your name's sake. I repent from all my wrongness and ask forgiveness from all my belittling that I displayed and stood before you. I pray for my wrongness that I have causes others to fall into their sinful ways, acting on my behalf or my misleading. I pray, O Lord, that my service to you be praiseworthy, that my open arms to you represent my love and devotion to serve you, and your forgiveness restore me back into the fold of your grace and mercy that I may walk in the faith of your love from this moment on. Amen

IN THE PALM OF DARKNESS

(John 12:46) tell us.

("I am come a light into the world, that whosoever believeth on me should not abide in darkness")

There are strange things in life that can cause you to go astray and fall into darkness. While dark clouds of depression are pressing against your daily walk with Christ, your daily living and moment in our life can be overtaking. Moments of separation and doubt can leave you with an empty feeling of hopelessness. All sin wants to do is hurt you and cause you to run away and hide from your daily choices. Feelings and emotions can become locked up and a sense of helplessness seems to bring out multi-stages of lonesomeness. What you may feel may shock others, but in your way of thinking, your lack of understanding pushes you away from the Lord instead of bringing him closer to you.

The Lord is the core of our beings and the core of our actions. Words that are not associated with happiness will disallow words of encouragement to exist in your life. The Lord sees the best in us when everyone else sees the worst in us. For the Lord sees you for who you are, and he only sees you through your ability to have faith and believe. He blessed our heart to love and be loved against the odds and through divorce.

Sometimes, we need to be pushed out of our comfort zone (nest) to understand the fullness of the Lord's Love and affection. God's love and where he stands in our life can overcome anything that we might encounter. Whatever you are facing, you are not alone, for the Lord sees a remarkable you. In our worse moment, in our worse hour, the Lord's gift of love is what he is giving freely.

Under great stress, dividing or falling he sees us for who we are. We are part of this oneness and beauty that he has created. His grace and mercy bring us closer to him. Therefore, divorce is not the last course of action that is everlasting but a method of bringing you into his full forgiveness and his willing to use you despite.

"Life is a beautiful journey without the Lord. It is just a journey."

Life is full of trust and truth, and a lie in a marriage or relationship will work hard in destroying the structure of the marriage. God's love always pushed us into what we can achieve. Life is a blessing; do not miss your blessing by not using the gifts and talents the Lord has giving you to develop. From now on, you should arise each morning with a smile on your face and love in your heart to reconnect just because your marriage fail does not mean you fail.

Just because things are not pointing your way does not mean it is your fault that your marriage ended. It goes back to the old saying just maybe the other person did not want you. There is always something going on behind the scenes in each marriage that will cause it to look at itself and wonder could I have done better if I had chosen another.

Thoughts of the past and visions of the future will never coexist but will remain out of order because of uncommon ground that was never solid in the marriage. Your lack of knowledge and unwillingness to see the true vision of the Lord has placed you in a bad position that will make it impossible for you to see or visualize your dream of happiness. The Lord had shared in your pain and hurt he understands the meaning of your divorce and how it had crippled you. The Lord seeswhere you could havebeen, and he sees a difference in your life if you had chosen a different route.

Despite all your troubles, commit yourself to doing whatever is asked of you in Jesus' name. Despite all your heartaches—let the Lord see you through them all and trust in him for your well. Beings, let him be the controlling force in your life, and you believe in your ability to lift his holy name on high that he will see you through, around and over to the other side of divorce.

The Lord's vision is not old for you he can see all you are shouting and praising his holy name. The newness in you is the old you are coming alive in the Lord, and he can bring out the best from the old. The Lord is just for you, and he will provide for your needs, and you can live after your divorce to see that vision come true, just trust in the Lord. He will be there for you in your palm of darkness (when something else is holding you).

"If past experiences have brought about a change in your life, you should embrace life and run with the gift of life, for the Lord has blessed you to move forward and through your circumstance."

"Keeping the Lord as the centerpiece in your next relationship or marriage will open doors of opportunities for the Lord to guide and order your steps until death do you part."

In the palm of our hand, we hold the fingers of our love through the touch of our emotions. As I our hand begin to sweat, and the moisture of our love pour out throughout our skin, we can feel the experience of our body reaching for its limit. Loving you has never felt better tonight, and I want this to continue to the morning come. Being faithful under stress can and will, in most cases, help erase the pain and hurt we are experiencing or going through. Sometimes, troubles and problems come in phrases. It is important that you understand that the Lord's love is for you.

In your marriage, there are issues that need to be addressed. In each marriage, there are times in the day, especially late at night, when you feel it the most. You must remember troubled times in a marriage are not a license to cheat or implied that you can give up and let go or walk away from the difficulties you are facing. Each day, God's presence should count as opportunities for you to shout and praise his holy name. Marriage was designed to be the light of the world and how things should be as one in Christ.

We should view each challenge as a blessing that we can overcome. We know what we feel and what is right is the best policy for success in our walk with Christ. As we begin to decode the sins of our life, we soon discover there are issues that we must face to overcome and bear witness to. In that decision process, our feelings and emotions can get in the way and create a lost and uncomfortable state of mind. It is tempting to judge a fellow Christian without cause, whether he or she is a good follower of Christ or not.

It is not your decision to decide who will be judge at the end of life's cycle. The state of mind can make all the difference in the world, but only God knows a person's heart, and he is the only one with the privilege to judge. A lesson for one is a warning for others not to repeat the same things or walk down the same path of uprightness.

To change, you mustplan by taking the worse of a situation and looking at it in a unique way. The faults of others do not have to be your downfalls. Looking for something good to happen to you through the arms or hands of others is not a plan for success. You must be willing to see your problems and troubles for what they are and be willing to step up to the plate and deal with it in a manner that will allow you to grow and develop into what the Lord would have you to be.

You must be willing to step out, step through, step around, step over and whatever it takes for the Lord to bless you. Repent is the first step, confessing is the second step and turning from your wicked ways is forgiveness that will equal your success. We are to help others who are struggling with sinner in a way that speak to their life.

We must show belief we can overcome mountains and that we can climb over or have them removed. By doing this, we can become a living example what the Lord can do for them that are going through similar situations. To judge one another is not the answer that the Lord is looking for in Christian living. We cannot be a God and judge one another then turn our back on other in needed.

We cannot just walk-the-walk or talk-the-talk we must step up to the plate and fight like a warrior in the Lord. He will be your voice and leg to move the obstacle in your life that will guide your footstep.
The Lord is not going to judge you because of your impurity and misfortune but your actions after the storm had subsided. It is at this point where we lose contact with the Lord. He has done so much for us. He brought us through that we do not need him anymore. That is our worse and biggest mistakes that we can make.

If your trust is in the wrong place and an unspiritual driver is behind the wheel of your life, you might find yourself between a rock and hard place trying to overcome hurdles of whirlwinds. We become self-immerse in our small state of thinking that we cannot see things that are foreign to us. We try to make amends for the wrong we have done with the wrong idea in mind. We self-destructed behind worldly things and wonder why our lives are going in the wrong direction.

Couples sometimes do not see the big picture until their focus on life is pulled out of perspective. We all made mistakes and pray that we do not become addicted or create a trend that we roll into that will affect us for the rest of our life. We try to create an outreach program in our life that will withstand trouble that we are facing. A reasonable voice speaks softly to us, and sometimes, we get lost in the middle of trying to understand our hurt and why. When you think about it is not worth your soul to hang on the sometime that is gone. At the same time, we can become dependent on self-control, but at the same time, we start toself-destruct behind foolishness that we cannot find our way back without losing the fight.

In the palm of divorce, love eludes us in most cases, this trigger our state of mind, and we become paralyze by our helpless thoughts. We find ourselves in a state of shock. When find our heart hanging on to every word that had meaning or sound like, it might get us through the day. We create waves in the actions of our daily living that we believed will give us hope and want to take our breath away.

We look at time, and time has slip by us, and we feel trap and powerless. At this point we become separated by our own experiences within our own creation. The river that flows beneath the bridge of communication and underline both worlds is in disharmony that triggered off we think and see things had they happen.

Actions are words put into motion that will result in understanding the movement or increase the power of one existence. Within those circumstances life is push to the limit and, in most cases, over the edge. Sometime, the answer is dim and muddy to the conscious mind. Your reputation stands out in a crown and bear no witness to your struggling and suffering that can leave you hope for a better tomorrow. There are days in the mist of turmoil that our love for one another get lost. Within the thought process, we wish sometime that things would just go away and never returned, but that is not the case of living in this world of unknown.

God's divine love is the window of true and divine love that stands for the growth of time. His passion for delivery can bring us through circumstance by giving us hope that everything will be all right. With his love and happiness, he is providing for us in our unseeing future. There are some many times in life we just walk around with our head stuck in the sand and wonder why we cannot see our future.

As we advance in life, we encounter many adversities and principalities that are more than willing to damage our life. There is no place that we can go to or no mountain too high or any valley too low that my Lord cannot see or see about you. As the wind blow through your life and storms of life mount up against you, holding on to God unchanging hand is the one blessing that you cannot do without.

As troubles in life caused you to walk on unsafe ground, it is easy to get lost in the debris of the forest. If your faith is anchor in the Lord, there is no reason to live in fear, for the Lord is a way out of no way. He will be your strength beneath your foundation, a stronghold that you can depend on that will be there for you day in and day out. If you must look for help in your trials and tribulations, let me explain that the Lord is the result of you crying out in the wilderness. Your cries did not go unheard or were ignored, for the Lord is more than willing to see you through the rough spots in your life.

Territories darkness is a concept that everything around you is total darkness, and there is no light to be found in any form, fashion or shape that will indicate there is no hope for you to see your way out. A discouraged soul is filled and surrounded by darkness, in some form, had closed off and push God's light to low dim that had caused darkness to cast a shadow upon the pathway that you are trying to travel and have left your eyes are closed off to the true light that is needed to see your way out of no way. There is a light shining on you to help you see your way through your darkest times and yet, you turned your back on it.

There is a light providing, and the Lord is your witness. The Lord sees unblemished love in your heart through your eyes. He knows you been hurt before, and you continue to live with the pain of yesterday. He knows what life have taught you, and your suffering is more than you can bear. He knows if sin gets another chance at you, your life will change forever. There is more to life than difficulties if you cannot see your way through them, you will find yourself sinking into extreme darkness with no way out. Sin is designed with darkness in mind and just that but not for you to live by.

If you are not sure which way to go or move, stay, stop, if not, the only thing you will know is darkness itself. What do you expect when your world is turning inside out, and there is no room at the inn for you to stay or stand? The ground that you thought were solid is slowly giving away to worldly thing. If you want your life to end up that way, then just sit back and let it develop without your input. A blind man can see if you give him a vision, a reason to believe, a reason for a future.

Sometimes, I can see well enough to recognize my problems without been kicked in the head. That is not a good feeling to have when the morning comes, and you are laid on your back. By that same token, there are other times a blind man can be hit with a bat that he never sees coming. That is the way it is when you are living in terrain darkness anything can come from anywhere. These concepts will make all difference in the world when it comes down to how you see your life and what it stands for.

There are few things in life you can afford to overlook or miss. Life can be afforded if you are willing to pay the price to lead. In most cases, you can feel misunderstood and lost. The lack of substance cannot stand alone if you do not have backbone, you might find yourself standing against the wall or window looking in. As the dark spots in your life ruled your existence it is easy to see your downfalls unfold before your eyes. When you are on the outside looking in, you can see the grass look greener on the other side until you get right-upon it?

In most cases, you can spot trouble hills that have the possibility of turning into a mountain which will grow and consume everything around it. If you are not careful, life can be a pitfall and ankle breaker, or a kneecap remover. Your false marriage with Christ can be at the breaking point because of your marriage with darkness that you refused to let go of. You might ask yourself why you keep traveling this disorder road and facing ground of uncertainly. By this time, you refused to pray anymore but always looking for a handout with your palm facing up. At this point, early in the morning, God is on the outside looking in, and what does he see. What he sees make all the difference in your life.

Disguised as it may sound, the real cause of doubt and skepticism, in most cases, is your marriage with sin. Sin will push you to your outer limit and cause you to slip and fall off the scale of hope. The bible speaks of sin in a negative way and sin can lead you in different direction in the marriage. Traveling with sinful nature can carry you out of the grace of God but not beyond his reach. This issue had been risen and brought forth down through the years. Can men be born again without the aid of a spouse? This question can be answered through forgiveness and repentances. This form of sin can bring an individual and its follower to their knees and possible an early grave.

If one refused to turn from their wick ways and continue to embrace the dark side of life, you will soon find yourself locked out of God's mercy and grace. They are only living and benefit in life will be their living and you can guess the result of that. The Nakedness of sins and the ingredients of misfortunate can misalign the movement of God plans for your life. Sin can and will in all cases weight heavy upon the burden of your soul. Sin will come back with an attitude amplified by revenge if left unchecked not once but thousand times over. Sin will come back with friends wicked than before.

As you struggled and grasped with the backlash of yesterday, commitment can twist and tie your hands. As you begin to observe those gods in your life you will soon find out they will grow and consume your life. Many sinners' struggle with recovering but, at the same time, become victim of their own belief and sabotage. We see this in many forms and occupations that have brought great Christian's to disgrace and to their knees. What seems impossible for some is a stepping stone for other. You tell the Lord your life story and speaking candidly about your disproportion in life. But this only leads to more confusion and misunderstanding.

Your actions to reactions keep you doing the same ole things getting the same old bad result. The very things that got you in trouble had caused you to overlook the very thing that is important to you in helping you overcome your shortfalls. You want to let go but you keep holding on to what you call your sweetness. The things you use to do keep popping up and the more they pop up the more you hold on. This only causes a person to lose their way and become misalign with Christ plan.

Sin is only here to confuse you and led you astray. Sometimes we refuse to try therefore we begin in fear of failing. Our confidence with ourselves can be easily expressed in the ways and how we look at thing and how we reaction to them. The weakness that confronts us daily is more than just a walk on the wild side but a daily journey to get back in God grace and mercy. These back breaking chains are millstones that refused to let go of us or keep us from moving forward doing our daily task of walking and growing closer to Christ. Man, dialogue with sin and sin dialogue back only to bring misery into existence.

Misery love company and have made you a part of its family. Sin can and will, in most cases, become cohesive and unbending glue that can suck the very life out of you. The word tells us that the Lord will make a way out of no way. That is easy to say but hard to understand when you are down and out and sleeping under a bridge, and your only meal of the day is Meals on Wheels. People can talk to you all day about looking beyond your problems and troubles but, at the same time, refusing to help you. Some will watch you crawl and beg but never help you up. Some will tell you about merit but never see your net worth.

Conscience Faults

1 John 1:9

"If we confess our sins, he is faithful and just to forgive us our sins and to cleanse us from all unrighteousness."

I had a dream that I would live a long and prosperous life. Then I found you, and everything was on the wrong track. In the beginning, our marriage reflected the thoughts that flowed from the spring of our hearts. Each touch stimulate love to come alive and sprung from the depth of our heartbeat as twin spelling out the letter of love vibrating through the corridor of space. Our love was talked about in the media of the community and envied by so many. We saw things as one, and with that idea, we created a world of our own, but they were not living with us.

When we speak of happiness, we speak about each other in ways that only the mind and heart would agree with. It was just you and me wandering the countryside, bedding in the roses of life. In our pursuit of happiness, we found each other with an open mind to hold and cherish forever while holding strong to our beliefs. We never tried to hurt each other with words or cut each other down with slain language, but we found ourselves doing just that.

We believed we were stronger than the world and nothing could separate us from each other. I thought our love would stand the test of time and our love would stay the course. Our marriage was built on the spiritual rim of Heaven, just beneath the angel wings. Our love was a bed of roses, both intriguing and smitten by each other's touch. If you saw one, you saw the other.

We knew each other's heartbeat, and love was the ingredient. We believed in each other as time moved, and our love stood still. We believed our love was unbreakable, so we let it stay the way it was. It was like the sun was refusing to shine, and our love was skipping off like a thief in the night. You could tell we talked and acted around each other, that their dreams were not feeling each other anymore. There comes a time in life that you find who you are, and those are the golden times in your life.

What you feel deep inside is all what you are looking for, and that is okay. You have found that someone that you think will complete you, and you have fulfilled your goals that the Lord has set for you. You believed you could help a man when he is down and out butcould not help him when he wanted to sleep on the ground. The road to life is laid and paved in both directions. In the twinkle of an eye, humanity start to take shape and give meaning to something more than life itself. Love and hate will become confusing and, in most cases, lose focus on the very thing that anchors love together.

The honeymoon was great, but tonight, reality hit hard, and the lights that once opened into a perfect marriage fell by the wayside. You started on the good foot, only to end up on a bad note, headed down a dead-end road to nowhere and took this marriage with you. I was feeling like a trapped animal in a tough situation that could not get away from or break free from.

I have known people under similar circumstance who are still trapped to this day. Lord knows when you need someone the most, they just up and walk out on you. Like a never-ending storm that keeps coming around the corners of your life. Like hills turning into mountains and valleys becoming so deep that you cannot see your way out. You are constantly wrestling with hurt that is turning into deeper and deeper pain.

Where struggles and commitment leave you with dried up feelings and emotions. When the light in love is slowly turning into darkness and, that darkness reflects the mirror of your life as close friends and family members know it as it is today. When you have not reached the point where you are not willing to let sin go, problems will start to mount in your life and trouble will come live with you. When you do someone wrong for so long, it becomes second nature to you, and you overlook the very thing that is holding the marriage down. I know what 1 John 1:9 said, but you were kicking me so hard and so long that the wounds are still open.

You were my sunset, my sunrise, and my world within my world, my beginning and my ending. Now look at me, I struggled just to make it through another day. Our marriage was no way heaven made or a box of chocolates. The last time we talked, I gave up the right for the wrong, trying to stand by your side. The things that make me happy make me so sad. Like joy and happiness, love is bitter and sweet.

I was living in both worlds, in so much pain and never feeling loved. As life would have it, I folded up my tent and got out of the game, or so I thought. We started to hurt each other with words, and it was always one thing or another being said. My heart had been hurt one too many times, and the memories of you are not fading away fast. I gave you all my love, and you treated me like a fool. The absented of your love had me running around in the daytime with a flashlight.

I came by your apartment Saturday, Sunday, and Monday all day and into the night, hoping to catch a glimpse of you. All I saw was him going up and down your stairs. As the lights in your bedroom came on, my mind started to play tricks on me. I was not your heart's desire or your king anymore. You had move on to something new, but all the while wishing it were me that you move on with. I would see your smile, but I wondered where you happy with him or if you were just playing a role. I had to ask myself, "Am I fooling myself?" I was not the one you called over, so I asked myself why I am putting myself through this.

So, I brought a suitcase and started down the street next to your apartment. I was not feeling it at first, but the reality of hurt hit me fast. I passed by the bus stop I did not have enough money to hop on the bus. Some of the drivers knew me but others were laughing at me. Raindrops were hitting the top of my head as my eyes swelled with tears.

As I crossed the street, I was hoping to get a glance of you through your window, but the only thing I could see was a silhouette of you flashing in the background of my mind. As he stood in your window, I drifted off into space. As my mind begin to play tricks on me again, my hands were filling with tears, and I realized the best thing in my life was you. Just because I stepped back to take a second look, you took that for granted and moved on without me. You needed some space, but you could have said so.

We just could not get it together, so I stepped back and tried to get a fresher look. I wrestled all night long with this, and this morning, you slammed the door in my face. As you were walking away, I lost my voice, and my heart stopped beating. I was dying inside trying to hold on to you. Let me say this to you: you ripped out my heart and threw it on the floor and walked all over my love.

Now, I am crying, trying to deal with my hurt and pain. With my headaches and heartaches in the same place, words were silent as I fight through and with yesterday's unhappiness. My life is drying up, and the only thing left for me to do is feel and hold in my tears. My mind is going, and my health is not in the best of shape. I tried to change my mind and have a good relationship with you, but as life would have it, I am alone tonight with nothing but hurt.

I found myself upside down in a well-known marriage. I cannot afford to make that mistake again. The doctor said I am getting better, but I need to let go of you. No one wants you when you are down and out. So, I will hold on hoping we will see the errors of our ways. I stopped to look around as I approached the top of the stairs.

By the time you found the underlying cause of the stairs, I broke down and cried. I could not believe my eyes and what my heart was feeling. What I was seeing was real, but I had to step aside and let it all go by. I cannot help but wonder what I am going to do without you.

History has played its part, and I have decided to move on without fighting about it. My life is too important to throw it away behind foolishness. I know you are a good spouse, but I need to start all over without being lied to. A liar in my life and lying in my bed is not a good combination to wake up too.

I know the truth about a few things, not a day ago, not a week ago, not a month ago, but more than that. You feel that I do not know, so you think you got away with it. I know I been sleeping through a revolution, and now I am awake to let you know your time is up, and you can move on. You could have had anything you wanted, but you were too busy chasing waterfalls.

Lying to me about a lie that I know the truth about is one step shorter than integrity, loyalty, and honesty. I know some things are impossible to undo, and there are situations that will continue to hurt if you try to repair them yourself. You brought back old memories like you always do, but you were not willing to step up to the plate and try to work things out. You can work your finger to the bone and walk away with understanding that is okay if you have a partner who is willing to work things out through forgiveness. Playing each other stupid is not the formula for success in a marriage.

I cannot change you or make you into something you are not. What chance do I have when you are holding on to the past? I must admit at this point-I wish you well as this letter ends and our marriage ends. We will start a new chapter in our lives, and there will be moments we will miss each other but we must go and turn the corner.

There will be no doubt there will be moments when I will hurt uncontrollably. Life is funny that way, and that is the way we live it. God will not be a fool for you; you are only fooling yourself, so you can take it from there. One day, you are living with me, the next day, you want to leave me. You got all your people in my business and things are not looking any better. I am done now because I do not have any more time to be played or suffer behind a fragile and fatigued heart.

Chapter 4
Not Putting the God First

Proverb 15-9/26

⁹The LORD detests the way of the wicked, but he loves those who pursue righteousness.

²⁶The LORD detests the thoughts of the wicked, but gracious words are pure in his sight.

Remember, God voice walk with boldness and with confidence that you are on the right path. Making up your mind is one of the most important steps in the process of considering leaving a relationship. When an individual considers moving on there is always a moment of darkness in the relationship that is in conjunction with weakness in the relationship. It is at that moment that we lose our way and converse back to old habits. By refusing to let go and move on, we become stagnated and lose our way because we are not accustomed to making wise decisions. We become displeased but never sit down and count the cost to move on and leave behind the things that are troubling us.

A moment of weakness allowed us to fall back into our situation that stem from yesterday. As each situation continues to cause trouble in our life and maintain an existence in our relationship, we start to struggle by holding on to our past. As we start to remember how it was and forget how we want it to be, it becomes extremely hard to separate non-sense in our relationship.

We start to overlook the unimportant things in our relationship that later turn into turmoil. This is one section or corner of our life that we sometimes refuse to deal with until we reach our boiling point, and by then, our love for one another has been overextended, and that which is left is more of the same heartache and pain. When we have reached our full capacity, we start to overflow, leave nothing but a pitiful life to live and combat with.

Bad situations should be a reminder of good times where the Lord had brought you from and blessed you through. An unpleasant situation can help you grow and get over a present situation because you know the Lord is there for you and with you. Bad situations should not dictate to you, but let your experience be a warning that you do not want to experience again.

Tough situation should set off an alarm inside your head that you had experience before and set up barriers you can bounce off. Usually, when bad go bad, this should open new doors of opportunity and be a reminder that relationship does have faults and downfalls. Couples usually turn small probing in their marriage into bigger ones, then allow them to spike out of control.

Should I go or should I stay, wow. When I think of you, I see never-ending rivers of love flowing through the chambers of my heart. When nothing else in life matter, where do you stand, and what do your faith look like? When the branches of life fail you, what do you hang on to, when your life is tumbling down. When your outlook is dim, and you are feeling helpless to whom do you turn? As sin continues to digest your life and leave you with an empty feeling that life is full of sad emotions. Who can you depend on and lean on for comfort to see you through it all.

You struggle day in and day out just to make it through you worsen times. There is one thing in life you can do to move over and around your hurdles in your life if you have Christ as your savior. Under pressure and within series of steps, you can find yourself trap within the four walls of your own hurt. Faith is the seed that give root or foundation to grow in the form of salvation in Christ.

Though salvation is free, and no man can pay the price for it. For the price had already been paid for sinners like us. Therefore, no man can step in and claim the glory talking about look what I did for you. Christ made it possible through his devotion of love and the shedding of his blood on the cross that we might have the victory. His love enables us to enjoy his true love of repentance and forgiveness through his charitable gift by pardoning our sinful ways. This opened the door for sinners like you and me to step into his grace and mercy. Before individuals can develop true divine faith, they must walk the walk and talk the talk.

God promise, and through his province, he has and will unlock the door to heaven and pour from the windows of heaven a blessing upon us.

When you look on the surface and a messing underneath, when your heart and mind is not on the same page, you can find yourself struggling just to make ends meet. Our freedom in Christ should show worship and praise as thanksgiving for our redemption through our daily walk with him. One of many steppingstones in the movement of Christ level of salvation is left in the hand of us. As we embark upon new understanding, we start to step up to the plate and move with persistence in the faith through our Lord and savior, Jesus Christ?

Saved by faith through the love of God, our reason was justified at the cross. The love of God brought salvation to a hopeless situation for our dying soul. The victory at the cross broke the backbone of sin and kept humanity from feeling the sting of death. The cost of salvation is free for humankind through Jesus Christ, which made it possible that all humankind be given the right to the Tree of Life. Nothing was left but to reestablish your being. Through this movement, man is no longer judged by the law but the through the salvation of free choice.

All blessings are created through a marriage with Christ. Gracefulness and mercifulness are gifting that God gives to help us to remain faithful through our trials and tribulations. This allows us to grow and develop into what God would have us to be. St. Luke tells us that salvation depends not on one is on religious heritage but on their personal response to faith. God does not want mighty demonstration of our intellect or power but rather the simple obedience that comes through faith (2 Kings 5:10-14). Salvation and deliverance from earthly danger and sin that seek out to harm us should be our daily walk to walk around and away from.

At God's fingertips was the beginning of time, and within that time limit was his word that stepped out on creation to become a living word. A word you could stand on and depend on to be there for you in your worst time. He spoke into existence the very soul that you have grown to love. Salvation required one to accept Jesus Christ as their savior even in divorce and through divorce.

The costliness of God's love is his abilities (characteristics) to die for a sinner's sins and give his life in place of. Divorce is no different when you have given your all and all, and still, your spouse does not want you. Divorce can, in most case, break the backbone of the marriage because it is designed to do just that. But God's grace and mercy is designed to bring love and devotion into action to bend a broken heart.

Now you know how the Lord must have felt hanging on the cross looking at his creation rejecting him. When your spouse stepped away from you and left you with a broken heart to heal in the only way that you know how. God's love at the cross unlocked the essence of life and gave importance to salvation, and salvation gave birth to your righteousness, and that righteousness gave the ability to ask forgiveness.

God took the impossible and made it possible for life to step from darkness into the light. ("Is 25:9 (a statement of salvation) Salvation saved us from sin, consequences, in the life after death, the saving from danger, difficulty, and evil"). Salvation is where God forgives man and creates the forgivingness network that generates a bridge that gapped repentance and redemption together. With each heartbeat, I feel you coming closer to me.

I never felt this way before now, sin can bring out the worse in a person. Sin does not want the best in you to come forth and step into God's arena of Love that he has prepared for you. Now, you must face the fact that you are no longer living a sinful life that is hard to deal when so much has occurred between you and sin. It was from the start that sin felted you and became deceitful; now the feeling is neutralize become of what the Lord did for you on Calvary.

Tell me this one thing: how you can mend a broken heart with make believed love; tell me, how can you change what you are if you are doing the same ole thing, the same ole way? Your love has spread somewhere else. I hope you feel good about that, if the truth is known, my heart ache for you, but I also known that we cannot continue our life in sin as a sinner. What you are attached to is more than skin deep, and sin will wait you out because your soul is at stake.

If you have too many hills to climb in your life and there are too many dead-end streets going nowhere. It is possible that you will end up in over your head. (That is the circle of love without the Christ), but we must learn to be strong in the word of the Lord and move in the faith of the Lord.

Everything in you is about the Lord; but couples always forget to thank the Lord for their experiences that he has allowed them to go through and come through. Dreams are sweet, but the story of life goes on and on. I am not dreaming of holding sinful ideas in my arms until the Lord come. I wake up in the morning with the Lord blessing me according to my faith that I am breaking free away from sin. The Lord has taken me in and blessed me in the harmony for his love and devotion.

As I address the letter from the heart: my heart cannot begin to explain the pain it feels. Most of my life, I have faced some difficulties, but nothing like this one. You can wonder why spouses move away from their love into the arms of another. Do they have more to desire or more than you have to offer? Therefore, you choose another to spend your life with. I know that you say love overcomes all obstacles, but there are mountains that cannot be climbed and valleys that cannot be cross because there are circumstances that forbidden them from crossing the constitution of law that state that: I do not want you anymore. No matter what a person thinks and how they think, if a person does not want you, they just do not want, no matter what you do to hold on to the relationship; they will always walk away from you.

In times like these, you need a friend you can depend on or someone that will stand by your side, but right now, it not you, you chose another direction to travel in. You found another to help you over the rough spots in your life. As life becomes a standstill because you are not during what the Lord had charged you to do, this will be harmful as you move into your next relationship without healing taking place.

When you are enjoying the company of your spouse, and you wish no more than to be with them for a lifetime but, yes, there is a butt, there is something standing in the way of your journey and something blocking you from achieving what the Lord has charged you to do. I know things are not right and life does go on after the storm. I hope you make the best of a tough situation and, change your wicked ways, and learn from your experiences that God can work things out of you. There is no need for this type of behavior or conduct to continue to allow misalignment in your marriage to happen.

When couples disapprove of their marriage and act upon it, their downfall should not come as a surprise. Like always, one partner is doing their own thing, and the other is wondering why they are doing it without them. One began to think there is nothing wrong and acts normal and believed everything is on the up and up or right course. Looking back at the result of your marriage, you cannot help but wonder what you could have accomplished together as one, but you will never know. In some cases, it is not your fault that you made yourself a regretful past, but you do know that your feelings have changed because of your spouse input in your life and lifestyle that left you feeling helpless and hopeless facing the next situation.

When you are holding hands with sin, sin can get a reaction out of you in the worse way it knows how. Sin will not change what it is doing to you and will not change a thing to make sure your life stays in turmoil and uncoordinated with the Lord. You cannot change your past or things you did before you accepted the Lord. I do not know if you are willing to change your present and investigate in the future to rearrange it to best suit your lifestyle. You cannot erase your past, but you can change who you are dealing with for the sake of your life.

I do not know if we are meant to be or can you live faithfully with your spouse. Can you tell me I do not know should you stay or let it all go? I think of the day that sin walk or make it way into your marriage. Sin will lean on you, and you may not see the shoulder level weight that is holding you down. These are the things that sin will do when your attention has been pointed in the direction of a sinful nature. Now, you have problems with others leaning on you and depending on you to be there for them. When you start to lie on yourself and for someone else about situation you have encounter, and you wonder why sin (spouse) had to lie to you.

Then you get upset and refused to put up with this type of behavior, sin have no conscious with you or around you. Sin in a marriage killer, and sin only purpose is to destroy the marriage concept and your life along with it. What you do in the dark will come to the light, what you do at the center behind your back should not be okay with you. You think it ok because you are the one doing the wrong and blaming someone else.

You should have known back then that thing just was notright, but you could not see it because love had you so, so blind. Now tell me how I can be so secure in loving you (when sin treating you likes a fool). I cannot keep holding on to broken promises and starting over again because you see all sins as friends. You know, repeatedly, I tried to overlook the pain. If it takes losing you for happiness, Imust let you go!

Not seeing the Lord in your marriage.

Psalms 115:5 they have mouths, but they speak not: eyes have they, but they see not: Matthew 5:8 Blessed are the pure in heart: for they shall see God.

A spouse should be able to see the big picture that governor the marriage before they say, I do or have some idea what they are getting into. A good perspective of understanding should be the norm of expectation that lives up to all possibilities of marriage. This creativity is a cheerful outlook or spin on the potential of marriage that framed the marriage in the eyesight of the Lord. Love should not be a dream but something you can wrap your arms around and put your hand on (your spouse). Not just a thought of words but action from words put into action by words.

There are small pieces of a portrait that make up the pictures of life itself. There is a frame around the outer rim of the pictures that support it. There are imagines that make up the marriage that can be viewed from the outside. These pictures should never be overlooked or taking for granted, but create a family portrait that the Lord can see and build character on. Because your marriage is a picture frame that the Lord can see and look back on and view, there is no reason you should not paint a beautiful picture of life before the Lord that you are living.

A blind couple was standing on the corner, leaning on each other, but what they were holding on to was slowly slipping away from them. You see, they were blind in their marriage to the point that they both walked in darkness. The things they used to do were far and in between, and in darkness, they lifted their eyes, they could not eat or sleep. At first, they did not see the Lord in their life or their marriage. They were in a situation that they thought would just simply go away on it is on. They could have lost their lives at any time behind foolishness, but they were holding on to yesterday's goodness that the deed of yesterday would give them new light, but they were walking in different direction.

They would chase yesterday with vengeance because they were remembering the past and refusing to embrace their future. They were afraid to create new memories that they could hold on to and cherish for the rest of their life. When hurt and pain choose to stay, it can linger with a fresh attitude on your mind for a long time and refuse to give up or let go. When couples refused to let go, they find themselves hanging on to the past, gave them strength to fuss and act-out of character. When neither one is unwilling to forgive or forget or look beyond their experience to move the relationship forward, they will start to suffer. Because the marriage is hitting rock bottom, you soon lose sight of the Lord and move without him. If couples never see the big picture, their commitment to each other will never be real to them.

If you do not set standards in your marriage, you will keep making and giving excuses for small issues and problems that keep piling up. This is one reason uphill battles you are facing turn into mountains because you keep piling up mess and junk against marriage. Marriage can be false as the days are long, and from the beginning of the word I do, you can slip and fall into a coma of the marriage and never recover.

Some couples recover from their ordeal, and others spend the rest of their lives living with the hurt of yesterday and never find or see the Lord working in their marriage. Because couples started off on the wrong foot and ended up in a dysfunctional marriage it becomes easy to blame each other for all the wrong that they are suffering inside the constitution of the marriage. When couples start to find faults in everything that their spouse has done, and theyare never at fault, they will start to suffer because of The Do effect that is living next door to ignorance.

Thorough you possess the knowledge and skill to produce a marriage that is worthy to be brought before Christ (and your love for another) is divine through Christ who strengthens you daily. When you chose not to let go of the past and let the Lord see you through, you are simply saying Lord, I got this. Therefore, your life is trying to find a resting point that will balance your one-sided marriage that the Lord is trying to collaborate through with you, but you are too busy blocking him out and acting selfishly.

You can be poor in spirit and act out of character by showing and holding on to your past by not letting the Lord work it out of you. We possess the wealth that Christ has provided for us upon his death on Calvary. The cross gave us the freedom to experience salvation for ourselves. The world cannot and will not offer you anything that will match what the Lord has already bestowed upon us freely. The Lord opened his heart and poured from the window of heaven into us.

There is a statement that rings true throughout life, and that is where there is no vision in a marriage, friendship is limited, and everything else will never matter or quite simple perish for the lack of knowledge. God is trying to bring your marriage into focus and be a focal point in your marriage that you can use as a tool to reach higher ground and build on. Your marriage to the Lord, with the Lord for the Lord, should always come first. Seeking his kingdom, all else will be giving unto you (Matthew 6:33). This also applied to your marriage.

To succeed in marriage or have a successful marriage, you must have a point of devotion. All points in a marriage must be goal oriented that everything works in its favor and work together to overcome any obstacles that might be forcing the marriage to be one-sided. Pitch dark offer us a moment in time that will allow us to escape into the depth of ourselves and be someone that we would not normally be. There are few things in life you cannot afford to miss. Missing Christ is not one of them. It is with great understanding that life has difficulties.

At some point, couples draw the conclusion that life little hurts and pains that remain are real and there for life. If you are going in and out of marriages, you will learn that each marriage brings their own growing pains. Some couples continue to fail at lite challenges, and others learn from their mistakes and grow from there. Experience is a teacher, and some couples never learn the lesson of life, so they keep repeating the same old thing and wonder why their results are the same.

What category do you fall into, and why it took you so long to learn from your mistakes? Are you learning or sleeping through a revelation that the Lord had given you yesterday. If your action is not acted upon, you will continue to keep mistakes alive and well in your daily journey. At what point are you willing to let do what the Lord asked you to do. The problem with love is that your heart knows the true meaning of love anything else is a substitute for the real thing. When loves to begin to die, our emotion become unstable and grows weaker. Our hands will start to shake and move in the opposite direction than normal movement around our existence.

We struggle with the idea that our heart is not feeling what it once felted. So, we fall and fall hard because our heart is hurt. We become non-functional in our marriage, and The I affect step into rebound mode crippling The Do effect of motion. Rebounding is the first and worse thing we can do as a first step back into romance. Just because things look similar and act the same don't mean it's the best thing for you to get involved with, beside that is, the problem it's the same, and you see it, but at the same time, you are blind to it because it is familiar to you. (You got to learn something from where you been to appreciate where the Lord is teaching you through your experiences, to know where you are going from your experience)

We need to sit back and examine the pros and cons of our past marriage before we engage in another marriage. One of the first moves after our heart has been broken is to try to recovery from our difficulties with minimum hurt. As we work with our broken marriage, we sometimes become victims of our own smartness. A broken heart will make you walk in a different space and time. Sometimes in marriages we create problems and get mad about it. But to the far left, we find ourselves fishing from the sea of unforgiveness that grow and come to be known as ingestion pain because we keep that idea alive and well within us. Sometimes in life, we create experiences that keep us jumping in and out of marriage that is going or taking us nowhere.

We used the blame game to cover up our day-to-day problems that we face. We point our fingers and blame our shortcoming on someone else. Our hardship and discomfort we pass off as normal, but we act abnormal by picking up unruly behavior and displaying it across the boundary of the marriage, which we passed off as blindness spots. Then, we never deal with our present situation but take them into a new marriage with little or no understanding what can develop from communicating our problem to one another.

There is an injustice that, in most cases, does not work in our favor. We get hurt in too many ways, and those ways equal to non-supporting attitude from each other. If you let sin consume your life and think nothing is going to happen, you are sadly mistaken. I have concluded that sin live just to mess with you in ways that you never thought was possible. This is why we get in trouble a thousand times over because our head is stirring in the wrong direction. I have realized the great blessing I have ever come to know is to remove myself from sins of this world. But I cannot do it alone, and that is the part I had to get in my heart.

Then I must put it in my heart that someone does love me for who I am and what I am today that tomorrow will not be this way always. There are parts and times in my life I was struggling just to hold on to my life. I was overwhelmed and overtaking by the absent of the Lord in my life. It was me that was out of focus with God's plan for my life. I could not for the soul of me understand why hurting was so painful and intentional. I want the pain to go away where my heart would stop hurting, and I would stop feeling the way I did. I was moving in the wrong direction, with retaliation pressuring on my mind.

Before I knew God, I only knew night as a playground for sinner like me. But let me tell you, nothing is free when sin is controlling your life or got you wishing things were better for you, but you are still holding on to yesterday's nightmare. I was having a suitable time at the expense of others not thinking about any kind of repercussion that might occur. The heart that the devil knew did not want you blessed. The knowledge of understanding that would make you feel connected to your marriage. The devil does not want you to beat him at his own game, but you will let him win if you give up and walk away from the one thing that God had blessed me with.

This approach leads me to believe that corruption and revenge played an important part in seeking out darkness to play my games and do my dirty work. But the light opens my eyes and brought understanding into darkness. Therefore, I understood my faults and that different course of action. Judgment and misery have led many to an early grave, they spent their whole life trying to get back at someone for something they did years ago, and they are still fussing and fighting over the same thing that brought the marriage down in the beginning. Sin has a way of inviting itself into our life and calls it home without our permission. For sin to move in our life, sin first must find that thread that hold our heart together. Sometime that string is our love for another and our wants for worldly things that get us in trouble, who have little or no value in your life or make no contribution to your wellbeing.

One of the most distasteful and heartless things I have ever encountered was and still to this day is an individual claiming to know God for themselves and willing to speak about the love of God in their heart but have no room forgiveness for others. A husband who wants to forgive his ex-wife and an ex-wife who wants to forgive her husband but is quick to speak aloud that the devil makes them do it is living in a foolish world. It is like having a one-way ticket and a no way back. Sinners are quick to jump ship and point fingers and it is sad to think and hear them say if it were not for good luck, I could not have any luck at all.

Fishing from the seas of unforgiveness is one of the more deprived and heartbreaking methods that can be displaying through human discord. More often communication between couples fails because sin allows them to misalign themselves on the wrong side of the marriage. Misunderstood leave matter of the heart in a bad position that can be display across the line of hurt. The Bible speaks of those truths to be evident against the human flesh that will quickly bring you down to ruin.

The pattern of ungodliness' begins with the heart rate. As life passed through different phases of life, couple learn that living has ups and down that they cannot count on. Before you let go most couples struggle to find the truth behind door number one of their lives. There are building blocks that restrict couples from being honest with themselves and others. When we confined ourselves to small thinking, we can no longer see the big picture or be honest with ourselves. Marriage with false identifiers will become traveling loophole in your relationship that will feed continual daily on your emotion state of begins. In other words, we become unholy and refuse to surrender our heart to God. We look for faults and circumstances in other people lives that we can control and take advantage off.

In this phase of our life, we backslide and link ourselves back into darkness. At this rate, the phase of our life will become toxic. A drug infection attitude played itself out in our daily walk, and our livelihood will begin to live under the umbrella of falsehood inside the marriage. A failure to remove old ways of thinking can and, in most cases, will slowly draw life out of you. Other social members and functions of the marriage will develop into a negative feeling if you let them rule your life or become unstable. Eyes that can see but are too busy looking the other way will fall prey to an unpredictable marriage. The way we are moving around and about challenges will create doubt that will enable us to see over or around our present situation if we are looking down with our head in the sand. There are un-comfort zones that will push out the darkness within us and place us where we can be free to praise the Lord.

"When couples see what they want but can't have what they see, they find fault in one another instead of seeking understanding."

Proverbs 3:13-18

Happy are the man that findeth wisdom and the man that understands. For the merchandise of it is better that the merchandise of silver, and the gain thereof than fine gold.

"If you fail to get an understanding you will always be misunderstood."

Love is more precious than rubies, and all the things that your heart desire cannot be compared to a want that is lingering out of control. The length of days is in her smile; and in her laughter riches and will honors your presence. She is a tree of life to them that lay hold upon her: and happy is everyone that retained her. Luke 6:45—Jesus taught his followers that one's speech is indicative of what lies in his or her heart.

With this in mind, we know that the person who speaks hastily is also hasty in his or her judgment. This is a recipe for disaster! Solomon counsels the readers to beware of these people because their speech indicates that they do not even have the wisdom of a fool. Wisdom is its own reward. Wisdom can aid us in many areas where our resources cannot help us. No amount of money can make you happy if happiness is not disciples in a way that bring about understanding and change.

Your enemies in divorce will see right through that and leave you with the feel of discomfort. You will be confronted with problems in life that cannot be neatly solved through normal methods of communication if your marriage is under continued pressure. Jesus gives wisdom that would continually show its value by giving us insight and understanding concerning how to deal with problems that would confront us daily while we are on our journey. During times of trouble, there will always be those who jump up and down and demand to be heard in their marriage, which is not warranted. We must listen with a discerning heart and wisdom that can lead to a value that is true.

We need to trust in God for Proverbs 29 reminds us we must trust in the Lord thy God instead of fearing humanity. Sometimes, we make decisions out of fear of what others may say or think about us. Others have made significant life choices out of fear of retaliation or fear for their safety. But Solomon pointed this out by saying that we should not be dictated by our fears.

Sometime couples married each other for all the obvious reasons and move in the wrong direction and wonder why the goals that they have set of themselves never bloom. They have dreams, but neither one buys into each other vision or seek to understand the plan that it takes to get there. Therefore, each dream is never fully appreciated or developed or fully blossoms into its full potential. Sometimes, we married for all the wrong reasons and pray to be blessed under the umbrella of marriage. When we misread the handwriting on the wall, we are going the wrong direction, trying to achieve something that was never meant to be.

They say, "reading is fundamental," I would like to add to that by saying that some couples hide their love inside the book of their heart because the spouse fails to read and teach from the pages of their heart. Therefore, love is lost in the translation, and only the cover of their flesh is read. During courtship, individuals can say and do the dares thing and smile about it because everything in the relationship is false. You talk about all the things that are important to you, but the reality of it all we speak death into our marriage and criticize each other for their shortfalls. When we chose wrong over right and act upon it, our movement, our love and vision for each other will become blur and if we never stop to get clarification in which direction to move in, our rights to move will be our own downfall.

"The I effect and The Do effect is the crippling mountain effect behind why some marriages fail."

"Most couples try to hurdle over discomfort in their marriage with their hands tied behind their back."

As we live to regret it later, we always wish we could have done things differently. If you refused to think or change anything about the marriage you might find it hard to get through your hardships and difficulties. Because some spouses never see their wrong. They always believed they are doing the right thing in the right way that will bring great honor and prosperity to the marriage if they continue to believe in each other without the Lord. By refusing to follow leadership through positive knowledge, any movement in any direction can be lost or poorly represented in the marriage.

The doors of opportunity within love may be closed and never activate in the hearts of individuals if they are never willing to give themselves to be loved and show any kind of gift of love. As marriage starts its cycle downhill, the heart and love stop feeling the desire to be loved and touched just to get out and stay away from the clutches of sin. I do not understand at this point why you think your spouse is more understanding today than yesterday if both of you are living the same old way. How can you live and not give each other? They are just dues when it comes down to the development and growth of the marriage.

By holding on to the past, there are things in life that are hard to deal with. This will leave you crippled and blind to the glory of the Lord, who can solve your troubles. In some cases, love becomes impossible to understand or process outside the covenant of God's love and marriage vows. When you are sleeping with your past and waking up with your past, the road to recovery can be hard to travel. The next thing you know, it is getting late in the evening, and life's trouble begins to rule your life. As time slips away, you realize that life is a struggle, not because you make bad choices but because you are still living within the composite of bad decisions.

Christians often forget that God is the Author of romance and the Creator of love. The world has distorted God's original plan for love and marriage and has put the focus on cohabitation and random sexual encounters. But as Christians, we can be confident that true love and fulfillment will be found in marriages focused on Christ as we begin to understand God ordained love and physical desire between man and spouse to be shared by marriage.

Then, we can read the heart of our love as a beautiful expression of their love to us in the context of the marriage covenant that was rite for us. Christians would say that their life has been ravished by the mere glance through the eyes of their spouse. This will allow them to speak the unspoken language that portrays their deep love for each other. The love of life will continue to be praised and given praise that will lift their spirit to new and impressive heights. Their love for each other will be delightful in living and giving their life for each other, and they will love each other now, always, and forever. Sweet fragrances for love should be a valuable source that is full of spices for the soul.

Marriage should be a standard that is healthy and full of expression of love between a man and spouse who have entered the marriage covenant with one another with the Lord as their guiding light. There is nothing like praising your spouse for their beauty and purity in the marriage. What is more refreshing than to know that the one you love is the one there for you through it all? Abstaining from sinning is one cycle that can be broken by bringing marriage under the covenant of the Lord's guidance. Therefore, couples are able to withdraw themselves from worldly sins and not live by worldly rules.

Marriages are different today than they were yesterday. The world should not dictate our way of life, but you are fooling yourself if you think this is not possible to love forever. But the word stated that we should not conform to the ways of the world and that we should operate and act differently from the world around us. Your marriage should be different from anyone else marriage because the Lord as put in place a standard just for couples that operate on their own individual standing.

Living in harmony with others is a fact that enables the order of the marriage and, at the same time, is willing to control the outcome of its decision. No matter how your spouse has hurt you and put you in harm's way, there is no excuse for retaliation. When it comes down to manners of the heart, our heart is still lined up with God's plan. We do things that are condition for our well-being but that is not the best results that we are looking for but what we can have if we stick with God's plan of redemption. By doing things God's way, we can stay within the grace of God. We can stay humanly blessed and not nameless or blameless but show meekness by showing mercy and compassion to others, including our spouse, in times of difficulty. We should live in truth and authenticity in a peacemaker way.

As we exhibit characteristics of the world, we become blind to what the Lord is trying to bless us with. I say to you to stay within the showmanship of your marriage to show the Lord you are willing to go the extra mile. If individuals are not satisfied with their spouse and continue to be angry with their spouse without a cause will start the process of longsuffering within the boundary of marriage. Marriage is subject to daily judgment that can cripple a marriage if communication is not part of the plan for recovering or covering the gap in the marriage. If you have nothing to look forward to, then nothing will come from nothing.

Any fundamental marriage should consider forgiving as a teaching tool that will stand the test of time. Everyone needs forgiveness so that each heart is forgiving to feel forgiveness. Who can live without forgiveness and let them speak now or forever hold their peace? The script for a living should be highlighted where we have to forgive as a formula for others who wrongfully misused us as a claw in their game. Your life should reflect the same toward others whom you come in connection with. When our marriage is hindered, and we reflect it through our hatred, it is easy to see where our hearts lie. But God pointed out that we need to forgive and be forgiving. Failure to forgive will hinder our fellowship with the Lord. Jesus gives us an illustration of how we should ask for forgiveness to move forward.

Through prayer and sacrifice, forgiveness becomes easy to do and allows you to move forward. Focusing on the inner characteristics of a person instead of their outward appearance will give some insight into what that person might be going through. It is in the heart of the person or individual that causes evil actions to manifest themselves inside the marriage because they remember or feel something at that moment they cannot deal with or wrap their hands around at that moment. The actions we often see and attempt to bring forth are symptoms of a greater inward problem that the marriage is internalized that is not being spoken about. Unrighteous anger, like derogatory name-calling can produce a hostile situation that can ignite an affair of the heart. This can lead to more anger and fuel bitterness within the marriage if not managed in a positive way. Jesus warns us as followers to be aware of our language as we display our feelings and emotional outbursts that surround our hearts, as well as speaking out about other affairs that govern the content of marriage if we have little or no knowledge of their well-being or condition.

Matthew 5:23-26 tells us, you will find an individual praying for forgiveness but is out of order in the Lord's plan of action. Jesus instructs this individual to get up from the altar and be reconciled with his or her brother before coming to the Lord. This is the same course of action that is required of us when we divorce and lead our spouse into the wildness of divorce court. In our heartfelt bitterness, we never ask for any kind of forgiveness from our spouse, and we just live as if they never existed before.

But we will turn and start a new one or get into a new marriage like nothing ever happened. God is concerned about our marriages because our marriage with God is affected by our marriage with one another or other (spouse). God is so concerned about our marriages with others that he calls us to reconcile with those with whom we have disagreements as we bring our prayers to him. Unfortunately, many times when we have disagreements, we attempt to take a shortcut and ask forgiveness only from the Lord. However, the Lord commands us to make things right with one another. Only then will be in a position to fellowship with and hear from him.

Holding on to anger makes the marriage vulnerable to outside influences on creep in and cause unsafe acts to tarnish the marriage. The feeling of bitterness and hatred can rush in after a divorce and set the stage for deeper hurt to occur. Unsettling matters are quick to draw a line in the sand and dare you to cross over. The dirt that surrounds your marriage is like broken arrows that keep the heart wounded.

Foulness does not help couples to avoid pitfalls or stop raw feelings toward each other from developing if either party is left with untold emotions or feelings that keep an open wound exposed to the surface of the marriage. Jesus reminds us that friends may not see things our way or they might decide to move in a different direction that can cause conflict with you with your way of thinking. But the Lord's Word is simple and clear: do not throw your moral out the window or throw him away because your spouse disagrees with you. Learn to work together to improve marriage.

Sometimes, our close friends do not show mercy or grace toward us. They offered us no solution or any insight that might help us to understand where they were coming from. That is why it is important that you choose your friends carefully. One of the best reasons believers need to forgive others concerns the forgiveness that Jesus has given us. It is commonly known as the Lord's Prayer; Jesus instructs the disciples to ask forgiveness as they forgive others (Matt 6:12). Failure to forgive others will hinder your ability to receive his forgiveness (Matt 6:14-15). The principle is simple and clear: no one has any right to hold a grudge against others because God has forgiven us of our sins.

Adverse conditions of the heart are the gateway to sin through the eyes of unforgiveness that rest on the soul of the individual(s) that linger around the absence of the Lord in their life. We must all examine ourselves and our lives to see the kind of fruit we are producing. Are we giving into lust, which will lead to adultery and fornication? Which, in return, leads to dead and ultimate destruction? For the wages of sin is death, so why go down that road when you know the outcome? We need to examine our hearts and determine if there is anything that we can bring to the Lord of which he would disapprove.

As our anger and bitterness get out of control, we must find ways to bring our actions back under the authority of the Lord. If actions in our marriage cannot be brought under control, this can lead to acts of rage; in some cases, even murder (killing of the marriage) will take root in our hearts. We practice unforgiveness, but at the same time, we hold on to grudges that can pull us further and further away from true fellowships with Christ. We must give our hearts a chance to heal by working and completing the Lord's plan for our lives and marriage. By doing this, we let him purify us so we can begin to show that we can forgive and move on and be blessed by blessing others who we deal with daily. Our ex-spouses should not be our downfall or cause us to fall into the pits of hell. Because we know God's love is possible, he wants us to give back in the same order that he showered us with his love.

Who you married make a difference.

Luke 6:43-45

[43] No good tree bears bad fruit, nor does a bad tree bear good fruit. [44] Each tree is recognized by its own fruit. People do not pick figs from thorn bushes or grapes from briers. [45] A good man brings good things out of the good stored up in his heart, and an evil man brings evil things out of the evil stored up in his heart. For the mouth speaks what the heart is full of.

Sin has a way of coming in the back door of our lives and walking through our hearts untouched until a mighty wind comes rolling in. Sin used this same method every day of the year. Sin will start a courtship with us on the simple thought that we are familiar with and not willing to challenge the heart. When we fail to see the handwriting on the wall, the fruit that we bear becomes our daily walk. By overlooking the promise of the Lord, we become self-destroyed. We move forward as we begin to function with unrest, and later, we regret our move. Our heart sensors tell us and speak against the move that we make by stating that we are lusting not in love but from the desire of the flesh.

As the dust begins to settle in a marriage, just maybe each marriage needs to readjust the standard they are living by and under the rules of the relationship that governor the marriage. The different between who you are dating and who you married makes all the difference in the world. Just remember one thing: if you are not willing to step up to the marriage, your spouse will be willing to follow you nowhere (not even across the street or around the corner). Who you marry makes all the difference in the world when it comes down to your mental, physical, spiritual, and emotional stability. The point remains that you and I are two different individuals who exist because of our love for each other. I am feeling you in ways that I never thought were possible. The touch of your smile, the feel of your hug, to knowing that you care the way that you do have brought immense joy into my life.

I dream of moments like this, where all my dreams would come true, and my life would be fulfilled by loving you. Did you ever think that your life would come to this, and the result would come down so hard that you would struggle from day to day just to make ends meet? Facts do exist within the normal limitation of marriage that put undue pressure on the marriage and can cause you to scrawl through the dirt of life. Society and religion sometimes denied the existence of divorce and refused to address the problem. If you fail to recognize your translation position, your love will show up as being disrespected. Some spouses refuse to talk about any problem outside the marriage or are open about conflicts that can resolve the problem by simply talking about it. Any spouse that refuses to address the issue(s) will find themselves in a turmoil marriage. Any spouse who refuses to recognize or not consider the reality of the marriage is looking for a scapegoat or a scapegoat within the marriage.

In fact, where knowledge gives way to understanding, the person who is involved may be capable of criticizing and ostracizing their own commitment within the marriage. Circumstance that constitutes a marriage may lead to suicide (killing itself) that controls the boundary of the marriage. The facts that your marriage fail does not mean you fail Christ. In understanding and reaching back into history, we can begin to see where divorce got on board and marriage got off track. When your love was strong the marriage was considered special just between just the two of you. The road was narrow and unbending.

When a marriage is only black and white and where no room for a gray area is, it is easy to point fingers at failure and shortcomings. A wide range of emotions that led to physical, spiritual, and mental abuse is not the answer that you are requesting out of your marriage.

This can go on for years before someone sees the result or evidence of it.

Two wrongs do not make a right. Most people are familiar with the term Sexual Experiences through Touching. These expressions have not changed since the beginning of time, and if the time for you has changed and you do not follow that course of action, you will find your marriage going through the mayhem. An important dimension of sexuality, interpersonal or sexual interactions, can occur between two individuals who are searching for their identity within the marriage.

Spouses like to be the object of desire and, at the same time, keep the home fire burning. Sometimes words cannot be spoken but left up to the individual who is a non-communicator to speak the right language to bring the marriage into focus. The unspoken word is the beginning of isolation that exists in the loneliness and depression part of the marriage that is craving for creativity from and through the non-human touch. Spouses are willing to seek friendship from their spouse that will create a warm affection that passages all understanding.

Only the heart can understand and seek out the non-human touch that it lone to be with (you). The supportiveness and sense of trust and loyalty must provide an outlook into the marriage that is workable. Miscommunication is like toxic glue that will dry up the marriage and create a non-value in a spouse that can cripple the marriage. What a spouse is looking for is an interpersonal marriage, not a commitment to the value or norm of life that is not willing to change.

Ones must hold a deeper value for the constitution of marriage that love means just that IN-LOVE, not a watery down verse of I want you. Love should be able to stand the test of time in sickness or health and be a foundation that you can build on and continue to grow and learn from. Despite life's shortfalls and pitfalls, you can pick each other up and move forward and be willing to forgive all circumstances that will create an unbalanced marriage.

If one spouse is yearning for closeness or intimacy, love will become unbalanced within the scope of the marriage, and the marriage will become invalid and unsuccessful as well as insignificant. As bonds between two hearts become unglued the lack of creativities and unknowledgeable issues hampered feelings of love. Therefore, it is easy to see hurt coming a mile away. As hurt and pain reached the surface and became a baffle of words and phrases that never should be said to another human being. I hate I married you is not the words you are looking for to heal your wounded heart.

It has been discovered that potential friends, partners, lovers, and soul mates are reported to be more difficult to live with today than ever before. Individuals had their own idea of how life should be and what life owned them. If you do not play a part in or fit into that role, you simply do not exist. The biggest fear is the fear of being rejected by the one you have given your heart to and love so deeply. The more you suffer from self-identity, the more you want to be acceptable in the eyes of social gatherings and social functions.

People of different civilizations and historical periods have engaged in a variety of modes or morals during their period of regenerating. Despite cultural and historical diversity, what needs to be kept in mind is that sexual awareness, children, churches, community attitudes, and behaviors are learned within Scio-culture contexts that define divorce that is acceptable in today's society.

Divorce attitudes and behaviors are a large social measure and non-cultural phenomena that stem from social structure itself. This is especially true regarding the issue of sexual orientation, which might form a difference of opinion about directives or indigestible marriage. This type of behavior can drive a marriage into the closet with great suffering mistaking. However, most divorcees do not agree about what causes the marriage to go bad or refuse to give a standard answer because they do not want the finger pointed at them in any way.

This suggests a complex interaction of biological or genetic determination, environments and socio-cultural influence, and free choice. Sometimes, our feelings are not clear on what we feel, taste, see and understand. There is a deflectable moment of emotions that crosses all lines of understanding, which can be easily influenced by individual surroundings (if they can get a divorce, so can I; I can do it too). You can rest assured that the facts remain. It happens. (Individual surrounding attitude influences).

As marriage begins to unfold itself, it is easy to become a victim of circumstance, as the situation dictates love turns into a nightmare. We all have moments that elapse and cause confusion in what we must do that is right in our hearts. These feelings can affect your lives and others who believe in our cause. By trying to execute your divorce yourself, you will find that problems are remarkably close to you, and you must face them head-on or suffer the after-effects. You need to seek understanding in a way that will ease the pain of yesterday while you are going through what you are going through so that the Lord may be able to use you.

Sometimes that is easier say than done. The raw conclusion sometime is not taking responsible for your part in the divorce, and finger-pointing is a major factor that surrounds most failures in divorce. When you are hand-cuffed to the past, the only things that will spring from it are hurt and pain. What is normal is abnormal and does not work in your favor. Sin is just that sin, and how you manage sin is the keystone that unlocks the blessings of heaven. Many things can be said about behavior modification in society and its function in today's market. When the norms of divorce are pushed into the face of so many people, the choice of life is not in the hands of the individual, but their faith is in their hands. The individual who suffers from the crises of divorce will find themselves in view of the devil.

Most problems in divorce can be traced back to human factors that influence the process that fails to overcome separation in a marriage. The answer is not always clear. There are too many factors that influence the well-being of a marriage. The human factors and environment factors are a great combination when it comes to understanding the product that can make or sink a marriage. Being accepted as normal after a divorce is an important part of coming back into the fold of the family of the church, how they see you and what they feel about you. In a moral society where values are looked at as normal, bad elements do step in or find their way into the recovery stage of divorce. This abnormal behavior can create a falsehood that everything is on the up and up, but divorce is a total mess.

When the norms are placed in front of church members, and the choice of life is taken out of the hands of the individuals, they walk with little or no faith in God. Because they are seeking favor in humankind and their private and personal goals for the Lord become lacking. Your faithfulness in Christ should stand out and reach across all boundaries of your life. Divorced individuals want to live in peace with the world, but the world is a constant reminder of their downfall. This type of behavior does not uphold the values norm of Christ. Any attempt to change existing morals may be met with strong opposition. Standards have been set, and sub-standards will not be accepted; that will lower those standards in the eyes of humanity.

We have forgiveness and empathetic sympathy, but we find ourselves sometimes downplaying what we truly feel about divorce, so we turn the other chin. Therefore, we use God less in our journey to recover and heal from our divorce. The treatment of divorce and its standard will be most likely to continue or become increasingly frank, vulgar, or immoral, depending on one's thoughtfulness. The missing ingredient, in most representations of divorce, is the sense of satisfaction and want within the structure of society. Most individuals who are divorced bare the shame or feel ashamed of others in their peer group or family, and while they feel at home in the church arena, they sit worshiping incomplete.

They try not to show their ashamedness to humans but fail to show their expressing in Christ who they are. It takes a lot of demanding work and praying in prayer to acknowledge how uncomfortable you are before you change and willfully accept the challenge of re-creating self into someone other than your present self. This level of responsibility is left up to the individual.

Divorcees and divorcers struggle with disbelieved and distrust that push them to miss the true purpose of God's divine love. They do not believe something like this could happen to them. They fail to untiring themselves from yesterday's pain and hurt by continuing to play the same role over and over in their next marriage. The stigma that surrounds the enticing process has left some divorcees or divorcers in a state of insomnia.

Marriage holds the idea that who they married they will grow old with until the day the Lord calls them home. But some never see their accomplishment come alive because they are sleeping through a revolved. Research has shown that if any part of the self is missing, then the whole part will become subjective or a trouble spot for the rest to follow. I have noticed that everyone I have interviewed developed a marriage with oneself in who they are and how they want to be viewed in the eyes of society.

Perhaps even falling in love again with the wrong person and reliving the crises that they just got out of. They fall in love with has-beens, character names, places, voices, and the likeliness thereof. Feeling deeply rooted in the American dream, divorce individuals believe that they can achieve the American dream by holding on to a part of them that wants what all America wants in their life. Most couple seeks and identifies with peace, family, love, and happiness and not feeling rejected.

Most divorcees or divorcers are afraid to tell anyone that they are not the person they think they are because of fear of rejection. I have found out that most divorces are afraid of experiencing the public's opinion but afraid to ask for God's forgiveness but try to work it out with God without his guidance. These emotions are an inter-zone dilemma that controls the zones between what you are, what you would like to be, and what you are now. You want to be a part of Christ but not of Christ. This predicament is hard to correct because of its complications and simplicity of texture because everyone has an opinion.

One's ability to overcome might shadow their inability to understand which road to take to get to the Lord's side. A breakthrough might be thousands and thousands of miles away, but you are crawling at a snail's pace to overcome their heartache. When you feel like you are reliving your mistake, every day becomes like a divorce, pushing you to the edge. Escaping to your own understanding is not the answer and you must realize that you are looking in the wrong place for a solution. This encounter can leave an everlasting impression on you for the rest of your life. A marriage can reach its full value through maturity, and maturity goes through many phases of difficulties to achieve its purpose.

Divorced individuals live by a full set of different rules, but these rules can line up with Christ's plan for their lives. Support is important in a marriage that is struggling to hold on to the trivial things that hold the marriage by the horns. The Lord wants you to step out of the closet and step into him and stop being oppressed by divorce. He can use you if you let go of the past by seeking him, bringing him into your life, and putting him first. The most easily available choice is how we, as Christians, church members, parents, relatives, friends, neighbors, and citizens regard the presence of the Lord in our lives. Therefore, others can see the true value that the Lord has put in us.

Blind Spots in a Marriage

Mark 8:18 Having eyes, see ye not? And having ears, hear ye not? And do ye not remember?

Luke 22:31 tell us that Satan have desires to sift us all like wheat.

Blindfolded is not seeing the world but stumbling around in the dark and confused as to which direction you should go. Satan will fit in where he can get in; if that means backbiting or attaching your spouse's character or reputation, Satan is down for that. One of the best ways to hurt someone is to slander them in their absence and, in their presence, say you love them.

The first misunderstanding in a marriage is overlooking the pitfalls that cause the marriage to plunge to the bottom. Not considering the risk of the marriage can be devastating. Most unsolved issues in a marriage are wrapped around patterns that leave the spouse's wound in disarray. This pattern can force love away from their significant other. Any unchecked spots in a marriage can produce issues in a marriage that will not be safely engaged with a closed mind.

In this unbounded association, most marriages suffer the compound damage of prolonged or unmanageable stress. At some point, Satan steps in and shows you your spouse and the things that they did behind your back. Satan will step in and tell you that you can do badly all by yourself. And that is what Satan wants you to think: that you make a big mistake, and you can take care of it yourself and live happily ever after. He can give you a point of reference that can lead to heartaches and pain.

At first, these blind spots are just those blind spots that most couples do not see until Satan starts to sift them like wheat. These unstable spots in the marriage can lead to unjust causes and undue pressure on the marriage. Without the support of family and loved ones, and friends and the church your social life will suffer beyond measure. You start to believe there is no solution for problems in your life because you are too busy trying to get over each blind spot in your marriage (words of emotion played a part in how you react to your situation).

But you are far from the truth and the Lord is the answer for which you are searching. Neglect is one factor that supports evidence that there is something wrong with marriage. We see what we want to see and the rest we overlook or pay no attention to. What we lacked in communication we fuss and fight about inside and outside the bedroom. Getting to know the Lord is a daily walk through his words of inspiration that will help you grow closer to the Lord. A crippled marriage or undeveloped marriage can have an everlasting effect. This type of marriage can produce a false warmness that can ruin a marriage if blind spots in the marriage or issues keep rising and not talked about openly; you will find life and living hard to do on any level.

A cold-hearted person will sit into motion a freeze that will demolish a marriage. As marriage drifts off into the sunset behind an emotionless circumstance, it will create a state of lost feelings or exhibit a non-sense of careless thoughts of their spouse. But a warm heart can understand the true feeling of love in a way that can mark a new beginning. If you face the truth and hold on to God's unchanging hand, love will prevail, but we as humans will step in and do our part by trying to do God's part our way.

Sin will corrupt your feelings and create miserable internal issues that will kill any desire of your spouse to seek love from you again. Fighting within the marriage can unhinge any dark secrets of the heart. History and evidence of divorce can continue to upheave any marriage that you might get involved with in the future if an issue is left unsolvable.

These emotions can awaken the crowd of insanities by producing a product that is not worth your love. A savage marriage can be stirred away from offensive terms, and couples can ask the Lord for guidance for their daily journey to higher ground away from downfalls. If the marriage is based on love, honesty, and trust, then you can count on loyalty to fight for love every step of the way.

If issues in the marriage are not dealt with in a timely manner, the marriage will begin to suffer. As the mind begins to undergo changes struggle between couples will turn bitter. Their living quarters will turn into a pillow of salt, and their arrangement will drive them insane and out of the arms of each other protection. These conditions will come and go as the marriage faces challenges.

If you notice here, blame playing its games, which might be detected, but what goes in the dark will become known, and usually, the future is not a good cover to continue wrong. As the marriage begins to show bumps and bruises from yesterday's hardship, days will turn into weeks, weeks turn into months, months into years and years into decades of the same old mess. Then, one day, without warning, your life as you know it will start tumbling down around you and your whole life will begin unfolding before your very eyes, and you will wonder why you did not see this from the beginning.

But to understand the full effect of the marriage one must look inside and outside to understand what boundary of the marriage hinges on. This is hard to do once the chain of communication is broken and left to ruin on the grounds of blame. Years will pass by, and you will wonder what you have yourself into.

At this point, life will turn into a rough hill climb and, on the back side, a downhill rollercoaster. You will do everything in your power to hold on and try to make things work out for the sake of your own sanity. The struggle inside your marriage is a short-term solution that can lead to depression and sadness, but you can overcome your difficulties through the love of Christ, who can strengthen you in your time of despair.

As life pushes you to the edge and leaves you feeling hopeless and out-of-focus. The real pretender of the marriage will rape and rip the very life out of you. You give through your heart until your soul hurts. Divorce pretenders act like they love you and care about you until you line up or until they can find that existence that will allow them to cut and run. Most couples in the middle of a divorce or going through a divorce will shout, scream, and take their frustrations out on their spouse. Divorce pretender will just up and walk away, blaming you for the downfall in their marriage.

As you begin to realize the importance of living life looking for blessings. Not because you have discovered a new you but because you have come to realize that life is more than getting slapped around and dogged out. The complexion of life, and nature of depression, and the shedding of nerves can create a deep and everlasting problem. There are a few things in life that you can hold on to and enjoy the fullness without sequences and pitfalls. The solution lies with you and the mate you have chosen.

When depression sets in, blood is shed. When things around you become un-plain life can become overwhelming around you. When thoughts of life are the victim of foul play and sequences of saying nothing have left you fighting and dealing with yourself. When the tears from your eyes fill the room of despair and hopeless moments are screaming from your heart, you are hurt from the inside. Sin had a tender to reach out to help you, but this kind of help you do not need. What you feed the body in most cases will make you sick and unapproachable, so feed it with the words of the Lord.

Deep healing takes place only when the spiritual mind is renewed to bring your soul in line with the Lord's plan. The impact of interaction uncovered the very essence of your existence. If the inter-the evildoers of a lessee's god have touched you, then you will find yourself serving a god of darkness. But to overcome the very thing you are trying to run away from, you must be willing to deal with it. Facing the problems and overcoming them is easier said than done. With years of experience and knowing how it is to erase the pain of yesteryears that led to the dismantling of the marriage. To be touched by it is to get help, and to get help is to do something about it.

"Some people are just natural born liars; they get mad and stay mad."

EMOTIONAL BAGGAGE

1 Kings 11:11

"So, the Lord said to Solomon, "Since this is your attitude and you have not kept my covenant and my decrees, which I commanded you, I will most certainly tear the kingdom away from you and give it to one of your subordinates."

Ironically, we spend hours and hours of our time wasted on attitude and how we see things from our own point-of-view. Our attitude toward anything that is abnormal can create an outcome that can cause us to lose our way and all that we have accomplished. My Mother always told me, "Son you got to make up your mind about choosing a spouse. A good spouse is not going to wait on you while you are sitting sideways on the fence. A woman who is known for their value and worthiness is not just going to sit around with you all night and day while you play around with their heart.

You cannot move with one leg pointed in the opposite direction to the other. You have to put your feet on solid ground, and you have to walk in harmony, side by side with yourself and show a positive direction. A good spouse is all about feeling secure and feeling needed in the relationship of the marriage. A good spouse is not one to carry around or keep junk stuffed in their tote bag or willing to keep mess alive in their life just to say I have a spouse. If there is no return on their investment, there is no marriage.

A good spouse is not going to let you lug or push them around like debris floating on the ocean surface. Their love is not a shopping spree at the laundry, mate. When you were dating, abnormal behavior was suspicious, but you allowed junk and mess to hang around and float. When difficulties are against marriage, and you accept them as the norm until you get married, then all hell breaks loose; that is your fault. Just because you fail to read the handwriting on the wall does not mean you need to keep paying for the base fundamental that you fail to read that reading is fundamental. When you marry that same individual, you become and begin to view innovative ideas of how things should be. This newfound knowledge opened doors for new opportunities to gain experience. You cannot be an individual that is tugging and pulling in odd directions, looking for a miracle in a sinful marriage living any kind of way in your marriage.

Nothing will come from a tote bag attitude if that attitude is allowed to strive in the marriage that goes unchecked. Life's sinful ways can derail you or push you in a misguided direction away from your blessings. This frightening move is just a move you should not have taken, but sometimes, we do not see the handwriting on the wall until it hits us in the face like a Mack truck.

It is so easy to find yourself looking in the wrong direction for your blessing. Friends misunderstand you and move away from you for insecurity reasons. My attempt is to impress upon you the importance of living for the Lord and letting your work speak for you. A blind man can see only if he is able to visualize and not be a victim of his own falsehood of actions. Sitting sideways on the fence is an expression that gives way to a confused mind that stimulates small thinking, and not being able to step down off their fence will cause them to fall to the ground or cause great pain in the marriage that will reflect upon the marriage for years to come.

Like an accident waiting to happen, you are subject to fall at any time or get off on the wrong side. I know you are listening to this or reading about it. If I am not speaking to you, you are in undamaged shape but if the shoe is fixed, then you understand where I am coming from. It is my understanding that life deals with us according to how we deal with life issues. If you are smiling on the outside but going through something on the inside, then you can stand up and be counted. You see other people having it good and others suffering just to stand, and others have it bad, others can cope with stress, and others have lost their minds behind foolish things, which is the nature of sin.

I am encouraged that the Lord will make a way out of no way, that you can stand and be counted and be a witness that life tragedy can rise and soar to new heights. When you cannot make up your mind about which direction to move in, turn it over to the Lord and let him direct your life. If you turn it over to the Lord and let go, and watch how the Lord will work it out for you, think will go in your favor. You will be among the ones who make it. Sin sees you as a prospect and is willing to go the extra mile to sift you like wheat. Sin is a veteran at war and is willing to battle you to the end at any cost.

Sin will rob Peter-to-pay-Paul and place your life in harm's way. Sin will float your life like a corpse wrapped in a cartoon of animation forced by the terror of yielding far from eternal stillness. Your life will feel like a sucking chest being thrust through strains of difficulties to maintain its normal form of daily operation. I was knocked down and awakened by a simple fall into the sand pit of life's disappointments. During these few moments, I encountered a low blow that pushed my life into a new lever of channels that brought about change.

I was overtaken by the warm embracement of sin that I thought was on my side. I stayed for a while in the broken arrangement of sin and worldly things that I saw each day that fed my imagination. I soon found myself wishing on a falling star and speaking in tongues that brought out the dark side of my life. Captive and motivated by the merit thoughts of having what the world had allowed my vision to be blocked by sinful thoughts and lustful deeds to spring forth, and my divorce was the result of that.

Sin had flattened me to the ground, and the weight of sin moved slowly across the freshness of my skin. I looked heavy at my new surrounding like an eagle sitting high and looking low at its prey. I needed to recover from my wounds and let go of the very things that were pulling me in. I was in hog heaven, blasting in the sunlight that was still huddling over yesterday's performance. I did not see the detail of my life unfolding before my eyes. I was too busy soaking in man's beauty. Not understanding the need of the Lord in my life and how I can overcome the troubling times, I just floated along the line of disbelief. I did not see the handwriting on the wall; I was simply looking the other way with my eyes closed. Even when optimism was possible, I saw the impossibility of that coming true.

I searched for deliverance in low and high places in my heart, mind, and soul that I could not rest until I found an answer to my problem. I know my love was being transmitted to different forms that led to the outside world. The Lord was so far from me that I was lost in my only ways of thinking. A desperate need to cry out from my circumstances blinded me from opened eyes. I could see the eyes of hurt and felt the imminent pain that gave me bad results, so I let them stay closed.

The thing that I was doing was not working, and I took a good look at Satan, and I noticed I was separate from God. I was surviving the dilemma of divorce like a broken foot, and my unhappiness came about from the loss of my best friend. But I noticed when Jesus became my primary source of life and my dependable lifeline.

I saw myself growing and overcoming obstacles that would have kept most individuals down and out. When Jesus became my focus, and my meaning became a purpose. I came to a crossroads in my life where my world was falling apart because my heart was falling apart. I did not understand it and did not know why. To be honored with you, I sit at odds with myself and in junction with my life that I had to make that change or die trying for I needed the Lord more than ever before.

Costly Sins

Romans 6:23

"For the wages of sin is death, but the gift of God is eternal life in Christ Jesus our Lord."

Open statement: A virtual woman should be the prize that every man wants and seeks. But every man is not going to appreciate what the Lord has blessed them with because they have abused love in a way that will still be costly to him to have. (Sin)

The devil's business is to keep you off track and twisted in mess and junk in a way that brings marriage and couple to disbelieve. When the union of love is broken, your place of understanding will become a sinking vessel.

"I love my spouse like the back of my hand, but sometimes I feel like cutting my hands off."

Many airlines charge you for excessive carry-on. If you notice, they always throw your suitcase(s) at the bottom of the plane. Guess what? That's what your excessive baggage is about in your life, your past, something that would shift your weight around in the background of your life (that which you carried around daily) in a marriage, which will cause you to behave in an abnormal way that can cause conflict in your life that is costly. At these prices live carry-on (daily handbags) can count to more than you are willing to pay. One of the most painful things about excessive baggage is your inability to let go, drop off your packet, or walk away from it.

Excessive baggage costs are factors or expenses that are unknown to the other person in the marriage until they say I do or discover it.

They carry around their garbage until they walk into your life and fill your house with their debris. Then, you must carry that same garbage around until you figure out what to do with it. This is after the fact you knew six months ago there was something wrong with their delivery method. They are always late for everything, always forgetting special days and have that lovely excuse for what happened and why.

You know now what life is about, and living with another is all about thinking about another. You had a choice to make and should have walked away and left your packet (spouse) at the airport with the airline in the (unclaimed department); no, you had to pick it up. You thought you would work it out, but now you know you should have kept walking in the distance, but you forgave. Until your home or house (life) or your way of living is affected by more garbage that you do not see piling up in your life, you walk with a tote bag effect glooming over you with costly sin in tow.

After all your difficulties you realized you walked into a marriage that was explosive and combustible. Connected to someone that you are constantly at odd with is not a good ingredient for happiness. When the past becomes your focus, your future will be limited to the experience that you are associated with in the present. You understand now that life has challenges and the lane that you are traveling in causes you to drive into a head-on collision.

Things you forgot to talk about in courtship or discussion prior to marriage are now coming back to haunt you or refocusing back on your life with revenge. Things you refuse to discuss and find a solution will look down at you and across your face. What is troublesome about this whole dilemma is you are trying to move forward, but you keep fighting with past events. Now you are living with the result of a difficult decision. As trouble begins to play a role in your marriage and as you struggle with old attachment, innovative ideas are hard to come by when you are living for the past that is living in your present. The past lies in the basics of your mind.

Because they want to play continually, the only problem is that sin does not know when to stop. But the flipped side of this is sin is not designed to stop because that is the nature of sin.

When you step into the door of your home, you do not want to feel your past rushing to control you, like a bad gentleman or lady of the night. You want to feel at home and in control. A home should be a place where you can rest your weary mind and feel at ease. Not a place of fussing and kicking down reminders of the past. It should be placed to sit down and relax for a moment. Please! You do not want sin to remind you where you have been and what you did.

You do not want that feeling of insecurity in your own home when everything is falling on your shoulders. When you do not feel secure, things can go wrong and stay wrong for an extended period. Like the past is putting you captive and pulling you down to its low point. This is hard to overcome sometimes. Unlocking those feelings of emotions can uncover the very thing that is holding you back and keeping you from being prosperous.

Many married individuals feel stuck living in their homes or at home in a cargo marriage where they are carrying the load. A potential mate appeared from nowhere, as it seems, but is bringing a load of yesterday's problems. They often leap off the page of your dream and flatter you with worldly ideas and opportunities to extricate you from your parents or previous marriage that is haunting you. They seem to have all the answers only to misdirect you.

Often, it does not matter to you if they fit or not, just if they are willing to spend time with you and move you from your present condition. Making a lifelong commitment is the farther things from their mind if they are getting what they want from you. It has been shown that most marriages have a common background disorder when it comes to long-lasting marriages. It had been showing that love worked behind the scenes to iron out any problems that might present themselves. The problem with that we (humans) overlook them and move into our own understanding.

Which eliminated any involvement that might work in our favor or show the ability to work out conflict in a timely manner if the Lord is in the plan? This time slot worked out in a way that reserves the right and diligence of the marriage regardless of how they disagree about the conflict. Couples who work out the conflict talk about the differences within their marriage, which may be causing the conflict. They agree to disagree about the continuation of the marriage to improve upon it. Any marriage that struggling to maintain is one that is in trouble with itself. One partner can trigger anger and resentment in the other that might bring the worst in them into ruin, and their difference often cannot sustain the marriage if forgiveness is not put in place.

Couples who have something in common can walk the extra mile in their marriage. Sometimes, the farther they walk together, the more commonly it reflects closeness and develops a mutual understanding through experience that can be expressed in ways that would last a lifetime. Spending time together cannot be put into words but can increase the commonness that encourages marriage to grow and become one.

One of the key ingredients for a successful marriage stems from understanding each other and reaching out to help each other through the good, bad, and ugly. Love has patience, whereas infatuation of love lives on the edge of destruction that is fueled by my urgency need to be loved and cared for. When feelings are gone, and love has the need to walk out the door. You will find yourself crying behind closed doors, wondering why this happened to me. When the zing is gone in a married, the predator goes looking for another mate who will and is willing to fulfill their dreams and thrill their imagination.

The disciple of love understands the true value of your spouse in a way that the element of love is present before you constantly. Love plays many roles, but the only one that truly counts is staying true and committed to your calling. The boundary that governs love is known as unconditional love by its name, and your name is written all over it. What makes this possible is the existence of God and the love he has for you and me. It is at these moments that we stand before him and between I know I will do right by you and moments between I fail to do right by you that bring the marriage onto the same page or push it over the edge.

Where forgiveness takes over, and love springs forth and brings everything under control. Love is no different from your heart that opens and searches out forgiveness through the words from your lips. It is that moment before that moment the healing process begins and ends with happiness in your favor. For the Lord knows you have paid your dues. Life is not a tournament of battles that you must win every one of them but faithful walk through them with confidence that victory is yours. If we are winning the battle of a broken heart, we must understand what is at stake in our lives and be willing to go the extra mile for our blessing.

The battle does not go to the strong but to the one who endures the race (or stays in the race). Some individuals only respond to life's pitfalls after they get hit and hills turn into mountains or near rock bottom, and they see no way out, then they say I made a mistake. As you know, sin will try to make the most out of its moment and, at the same time, ruin your marriage with Christ. The only way this can happen is if you let sin rule your life and circumstances by standing back. This is the same method he imports into your marriage, for he knows that you are struggling with doubt, and his best move is to keep it that way and keep your eyes and heart somewhere else; that way, you never see sin coming to harm you around my atomic makeup that surrounded my rapid decline in life's pitfalls.

The accumulating of sins in my life left evidence of clinical helplessness that forced me into moments of need. Sin played a large part in life's transformation into and out of the blessing of God. Not only is sin tall but round and heavy in your life to the point of being deadly overweight. When sin is distrustful, who can you put your faith in that will allow you to move in a positive direction? You cannot determine your path; therefore, the Lord orders your steps. You mark your lifestyle carefully and hide your face to reveal nothing that gives way to your hurt. You keep a gaze fixed on your face and captivate the minds of others to reveal nothing but an occasionally blinked in your life. Some sinners reap what they sow very slowly. Some sinner closes their eyes momentarily to rest, never to awaken to realize their full potential because they have been sleeping through a revelation in the marriage.

If the Lord sees inside your heart

Would he see anything that looks beautiful?

Would he see a seed blossoming from the seat of love?

Would he see the falsehood of lies in the heart vessel of your eyes?

A vision that you cannot see but hidden inside.

A thought that is blurred but speaking from hidden places.

SCRIPTURE REFERENCES:

All scripture reference was taken from the King James Version of the bible public domain.

OTHER STUDIES:

Amos 3:3 (KJV)

Can two walk together, except they be agreed?